HOME-MADE
WINES,
CORDIALS
& SYRUPS

WI
LIFE & LEISURE

HOME-MADE

WINES, CORDIALS & SYRUPS

Dr F. W. Beech

WI BOOKS LTD

Acknowledgements

Editor Suzanne Luchford
Commissioning Editor Hilary Wharton
Line illustrations by Antonia Enthoven and Simon Roulstone
Picture research Julia Golding
Photographs Paul Freestone except pages 17 above Wood/Image Bank,
below Smith Collection; 65 above and 145 G. Buntrock/Anthony
Blake; 97 Patrick Eager
Cover photography Jhon Kevern
Designed by Anita Ruddell
Equipment courtesy of Boisdale Wines, The Boots Company Ltd,
Elizabeth David and David Mellor.
This edition produced by Ward Lock (Publishers) Ltd,
8 Clifford Street, London W1X 1RB, an Egmont Company

Published by WI Books Ltd
39 Eccleston Street
London SW1W 9NT

British Library Cataloguing in Publication Data

Beech, F.W. (Frederick Walter)
Home-made wines, cordials & syrups.
1. Wines. Recipes
I. Title   II. Series
641.8'72
ISBN 0-947990-35-6

First published 1954
Revised and updated 1988
© WI Books Ltd 1988

Text set in Goudy Old Style by Hourds Typographica, Stafford
Colour reproduction by Tennon and Polert Colour Scanning Ltd,
Hong Kong
Printed and bound in Great Britain by
Hazell, Watson & Viney Ltd,
Member of the BPCC Group, Aylesbury, Bucks

WI Life & Leisure Series
The Complete Book of Home Preserving by Mary Norwak

LIST OF CONTENTS

INTRODUCTION

*F*or centuries wine-making and the preparation of syrups and cordials were common practices in all homes, whether cottages or country mansions. The recipes were handed down through the generations and some of the recipe books still exist, either in manuscript or in book form from later publications. These practices lapsed during the Second World War because of sugar shortages, but began to revive in the early 1950s as the result of the general shortage of wine and the high excise duties.

At the beginning of the 1950s the WI, with its tradition of encouraging home crafts and skills, asked members for copies of family recipes. Some of these recipes, by their reference to sugar candy and large additions of brandy, went back to the heyday of home wine-making. Others had been copied from books or were old extracts from local newspapers. A selection of the best recipes and some simple instructional chapters appeared in 1954. Since then the popularity of the topic has increased, reflected by the growing number of amateur wine-making societies and the development of specialised equipment. The original book went through several revisions to include the newer scientific methods for home wine-making and the use of concentrates and kits. The present book is based on these editions and has been thoroughly revised and up-dated.

• USING THE BOOK •

This book has been divided into two main sections – instructional chapters and recipe chapters. The instructional chapters explain the basic principles in some detail and should be referred to when in doubt about a particular point.

The recipes utilise not only raw materials from the garden and market but also from the hedgerow. When collecting from the countryside, it is useful to have a simple book on the identification of wild flowers and shrubs. There are also commercial concentrated and single strength juices, and dried fruits that can be used. Details of these appear in the recipe chapters. Beginners, if they wish, can start with the recipe chapters provided they read the introduction to the relevant chapter. Advice on any problems experienced is given in Problems of Wine-Making (page 148). With practice, recipe variations can be developed that suit each maker's palate.

Every home wine-maker has two legal obligations. Home-produced wines can be made tax and duty-free and without a licence provided they are not sold. They cannot be given away for sale, whether this is private, at public sales, produce exhibitions or a WI Market.

The second is even more important. No attempt should ever be made to distil any alcoholic beverage in the home. The ban also applies to increasing the alcoholic strength by removal of water as ice (the Alcoholic Liquor Duties Act, 1979). Not only does distillation contravene the law, it is also quite possible to go blind after drinking the resulting distillate, since it can contain excessive methyl alcohol.

When alcoholic strength is quoted it is per cent by volume.

NOTES ON METRIC &
• IMPERIAL MEASUREMENTS •

All measurements are given in metric and imperial units. Never mix metric and imperial, follow one system only as the two are not interchangeable. The quantity of wine produced in each recipe is based on five litres and one gallon.

TYPES OF
WINE

Decide on the type of wine you wish to produce before you begin. Nearly all the commercial wine styles can be made at home. Red and white wines can be made from red grapes with suitable treatment but otherwise the colour of the wine is dictated by the raw material. Fresh fruits, dried fruits, vegetables, flowers, cereals and many others can be used. An indication is given with each recipe of the type of wine produced.

The classification of wines used in wine competitions (given below) is useful for summarising wine types.

Aperitif A wine drunk by itself before a meal to stimulate the appetite. It can be dry or sweet, sometimes bitter and not more than 14–16 per cent alcohol. Aperitifs are often drunk chilled.

Table Wine A wine that is suitable for accompanying and enhancing the flavour of meal. Generally it is not too strong in flavour or aroma, with an alcohol content of 10–12 per cent. It is usually dry, or slightly sweet and lighter in body than a social wine.

Dessert (Sweet) Wine Served with the dessert course or after a meal; it is full flavoured, medium to sweet and has an alcoholic content of 15–20 per cent. It can be white, shades of fawn, brown or tawny or red.

Social Wine One of the most popular types of home-made wine usually drunk other than at a meal. Its composition is between a table and dessert wine and its alcohol content is about 14 per cent.

Country Wine A term used in this book for a full-bodied, robust flavoured sweet wine which is often spiced. Its alcohol content is about 16 per cent. It is often made using a traditional recipe without modern ingredients such as pectic enzyme, unless absolutely necessary.

Rosé Wine Should be pink in colour, with a delicate aroma and flavour, sometimes slightly sparkling. It contains about 10 per cent alcohol and can be served at almost any time.

Sparkling Wine This wine should contain carbon dioxide produced by secondary fermentation in the bottle. It can be white, pink or even red, and drunk on any occasion. It contains about 10 per cent alcohol.

• QUALITY •

All wines should be clean, fresh in flavour and free from faults. The flavour of the raw material should not be overpowering. Whether sweet or dry on the palate, the sweetness, acidity and any bitterness or astringency should all be in balance when the wine is tasted. An excess of one of these qualities spoils the enjoyment of the wine almost as much as a taint. Old recipes often involved spicing, presumably to hide any imperfections in the wine.

Flavour balance is a matter of personal taste, although at wine competitions there are recognised standards. Each wine-maker learns to find his or her own preference by making and drinking different types of wine. Help is now available from a number of major wine retailers who classify their white wines according to degree of sweetness and red wines to depth of flavour. Buying and tasting examples from different classes will give a good idea of the preferred flavour balance.

With experience, home wine-makers can give personal quality ratings to their wines and modify recipes to remedy flavour deficiences. The test of expertise is winning prizes at amateur wine competitions. These are organised throughout the country each year by the federations of wine societies. There is also an annual national show run by the National Association of Wine and Beer Makers. Such competitions are judged by the National Guild of Wine and Beer Judges and by judges appointed by the various regional federations.

EQUIPMENT

Purpose-made equipment is widely available from home-brew centres, chemists and many other outlets. It is light, easy to clean and long lasting. Once you have decided to make wine regularly it is worth buying a wider range of equipment. In 'acquiring' items, anything with copper, iron, lead or zinc (galvanised) surfaces must be avoided as these materials spoil the colour and flavour of the product and damage the health of the consumer. Avoid resinous or coniferous wood, highly coloured plastics or ancient glazed or enamelled ware. *Never* use any container that has previously held anything other than a beverage.

· ESSENTIAL EQUIPMENT ·

Chopping board and sharp stainless steel knife (or a chef's hatchet) for slicing tough material.

Hand grater or slicer, kitchen grinder, potato masher or a mallet for the same purpose.

Colander for washing and draining the raw material.

Measures Graduated jug, measuring cylinders and kitchen scales.

Bowl A bowl, bin and/or bucket for the early stages of extraction or fermentation.

Hydrometer and jar for measuring the sugar content (specific gravity) of the juices and fermenting and stored wines.

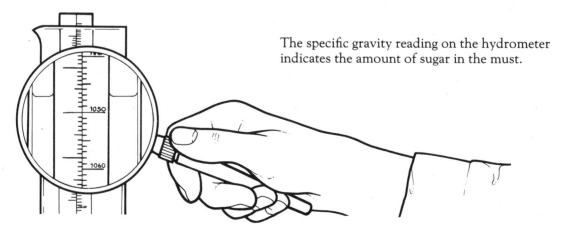

The specific gravity reading on the hydrometer indicates the amount of sugar in the must.

Cloths Close textured knitted nylon or terylene, for squeezing liquid out of pulp. Coarse and fine nylon straining bags are also available. A fine sieve can be used for removing small particles.

Glass jars, plastic bins or rigid plastic barrels for the main fermentation and later for storing wine.

Air-lock in glass or plastic, each with a bored rubber cork for inserting in the neck of a fermenting vessel. A small quantity of water or sulphite solution is put into the gadget to form the actual lock. Gas coming from the fermentation is able to push its way through the water, but the air from the atmosphere is prevented from getting into the jar.

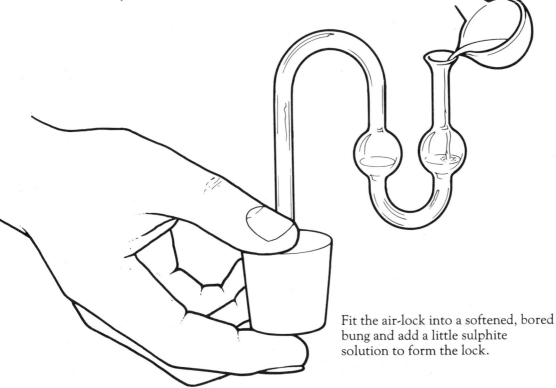

Fit the air-lock into a softened, bored bung and add a little sulphite solution to form the lock.

Syphon Usually made of pliable plastic tubing, it can be bought fitted with a tap and other small refinements. Essential for 'racking' or syphoning the wine clear of the yeast deposit.

Bottles New or second-hand wine bottles for still wines. True champagne bottles for sparkling wines. Strong 300 ml/$\frac{1}{2}$ pint bottles for syrups. Bottle brushes are very useful for removing internal deposits during cleaning.

Corks and Stoppers Straight-sided bark corks and flanged stoppers for wines and syrups. Inexpensive hand corking machines can be bought. Plastic stoppers can be re-used after sterilising. Preformed wires and muslets are available for securing corks in bottles of sparkling wines. There is a simple hand held device for crimping crown corks on bottles.

Funnel A wide-mouthed plastic funnel is a great help when transferring wines from jar to jar or to bottles.

Waterbath, kettle or preserving pan Needed for sterilising bottled juices and syrups.

Stirrer or spoon Wooden or plastic, for mixing.

• LABOUR SAVING EQUIPMENT •

Boiler Holding between 15–25 litres/3.3–5.5 gallons is invaluable for providing sufficient hot water for hot extraction of pulp and for washing bottles.

Grinder/crusher, food processor and liquidiser For pulping large quantities of fruit there is the Pulpmaster which has a stainless steel blade on a long spindle. The coarsely chopped raw material is put in a bucket and

Many fruits can be prepared for wine-making by using a liquidiser or food processor.

the blade inserted. The spindle is passed through a hole in the lid of a bucket which is pressed into place. With an electric drill secured to the end of the spindle, the material is rapidly pulped. Specialist suppliers have purpose-built hand or electrically operated crushers for processing large quantities of fruit and vegetable in the home. Many fruits can be pulped using a food processor or liquidiser.

Presses These range from the small, enamelled presses through to basket presses of increasing size in which pressure is applied with a screw or rachet.

Steam extractor An alternative to the press. A few kilos of fruit or vegetable, chopped roughly, are extracted with steam. A large gas ring ensures that sufficient steam is generated quickly.

Fermentation heaters Fermentations may cease during the winter because the ambient temperature is too low; it is sometimes difficult to restart them. There are now thermostatically controlled electric immersion heaters (miniature), heating trays or jar jackets available.

Filtration It is possible to make very clear wines without filtration. Sometimes a fining agent (Problems of Wine-Making page 148) is also used. A wine filter is necessary if a wine-maker is in a hurry, or a perfectionist, or enters wine competitions seriously. Filters range from a pleated filter paper in a funnel to filter kits. Filtration can be improved if filter powders or crystals are added.

Safety bungs Fitted to jars of stored wines, they automatically release any gas pressure from secondary fermentation and so avoid explosions.

Dressing the bottles Labels, capsules (crimped or self-shrinking) improve the appearance of wine when bottles are brought to the table.

Record cards or wine log For keeping records of each batch of wine made.

CLEANING & STERILISING

All equipment must be kept scrupulously clean when not in use, as otherwise moulds and other spoilage organisms will grow on any residues and spoil the next batch of wine. If domestic detergents and brushing fail to remove encrusted deposits, there are several excellent products on the market which will do this. Soak the equipment in the solution as directed by the manufacturer. Alternatively, use a strong solution of domestic bleach (5 ml/1 fl oz bleach per 1 litre/1 gallon of water).

After cleaning, the equipment has to be sterilised. Commercial preparations are available but it is easy to make an SO_2 *sterilising solution* using one of the methods below.

1 Dissolve six Campden tablets and 15 g/½ oz citric acid in 600 ml/1 pint of water.
2 Dissolve 1½ g/¼ oz of sodium (or potassium) metabisulphite and citric acid in 1 litre/1 gallon of water *or*
3 Dissolve a large pinch of each in 600 ml/1 pint of water.
4 Dissolve 150 g/6 oz sodium metabisulphite in 2 litres/½ gallon of water, add 2 tbsp of citric acid and make up to 5 litres/1 gallon.

These solutions are quite stable and can be used several times before discarding. They should be kept in stoppered containers and well out of the way of children. Handle them with care as the fumes can irritate the nose, eyes, and throat. Sufferers from respiratory ailments should be particularly careful. Use the solutions in a well ventilated room, or in the open air. Never add them to juice or wine.

· STERILISING EQUIPMENT ·

Containers (jars, bins) can be left after cleaning with about 1 cm/½ in. of sterilising solution in the bottom and sealed. When required, drain and re-use.

Bottles Before filling with wine, pour a small quantity of SO_2 sterilising solution into each bottle. Insert a bung, rotate to cover all the inner

Sterilise the fermentation vessel by leaving 1 cm/$\frac{1}{2}$ in. sterilising solution in the bottom and seal. When required, drain and re-use. Attention to cleanliness prevents problems later.

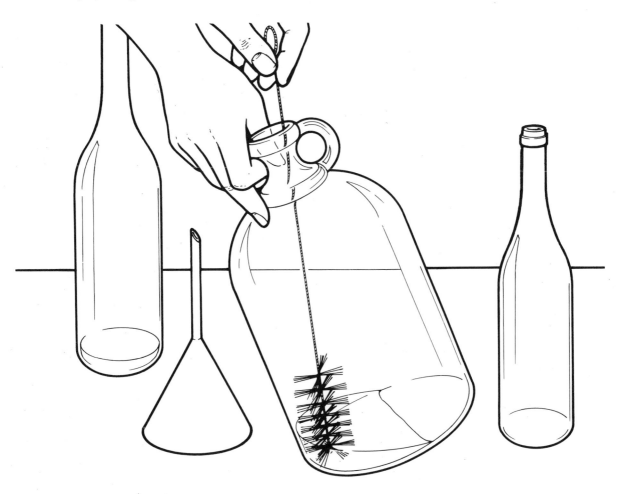

surface. Remove the bung and pour the solution into the next bottle. Allow bottles to drain before filling with wine.

Corks Should be softened as well as sterilised before use. Keep them submerged in cold water for 24 hours, drain and rinse with a little of the SO_2 sterilising solution. Drain a few corks at a time before use, otherwise they will dry out and be hard to drive into the necks of bottles.

Small items Rinse syphons well, insert a small funnel into one end and run a little SO_2 sterilising solution through and back into its storage bottle.

Filters Wash the equipment thoroughly, rinse with a little of the SO_2 sterilising solution and drain dry.

BASIC ESSENTIALS OF SUCCESSFUL WINE-MAKING

The basic principles of successful wine-making are simple. Wine-making consists of pre-treating a raw material to extract flavour and then adding a selective sterilising agent (usually sulphur dioxide) to destroy spoilage yeasts and bacteria. When the sterilising agent has completed its action, a yeast culture is added to ferment the sugar, forming alcohol, carbon dioxide and more flavour components. Hence the requirements are:

1 Good quality raw materials.
2 Enough fermentable sugar to give the required alcohol content and final degree of sweetness.
3 Enough acidity to assist the action of the added sulphur dioxide and for good flavour balance.
4 The addition of the optimum amount of sulphur dioxide.
5 A juice extraction method that retains the desired flavour qualities in the wine.
6 Fermentation conditions that allow the steady conversion of sugar to alcohol and flavour components by the added yeast.
7 Stabilisation of the wine after fermentation and prior to bottling to prevent unwanted changes in colour, clarity and flavour.
8 Correct pre-treatment to prevent uncontrolled fermentation in the bottle.
9 Controlled secondary fermentation is essential when making sparkling wines.
10 *General:* impervious surfaces for all equipment in contact with the raw materials, juice/extract, wine; effective cleaning and sterilisation methods for maintaining a good standard of hygiene at all times.

Above: A selection of the different types of bottles suitable for wine-making. *Below:* The essential equipment for home wine-making is readily available from home-brew centres and chemists.

RAW
MATERIALS

· SAFETY ·

Wines can be made from a wide variety of plant parts. Those given in the recipes are quite safe to use. Every plant and every part of a plant which is not positively known to be edible should be considered as potentially hazardous. In case of doubt consult the *Ministry of Agriculture Fisheries and Food Bulletin No 161, British Poisonous Plants* by A.A. Forsyth.

The origins of the raw materials used in wine-making are important. Those gathered from your own garden are normally free of chemical spray residues. Produce from pick-your-own farms and orchards, grocers and wholesale markets conform to minimum spray residue regulations. Ideally, try and set aside any raw materials in your garden to be used for wine-making and leave these unsprayed. If spraying is necessary, use chemicals recommended as safe for food-stuffs so that the raw material can be eaten 24 hours after spraying.

When picking raw material from hedgerows, avoid places where weed killers have obviously been used. Any fruits and leaves growing alongside roads will contain a higher than normal lead content from car exhaust fumes. Washing will not remove enough of the residues so avoid materials from such sites.

Fresh material should be gathered on a dry day after any dew has evaporated. This will prevent the rapid growth of moulds, especially in delicate flowers. The produce should be free of insect infestation and obvious mould growth or rots. It should be ripe, but not over-ripe, with the possible exceptions of hips, haws and medlars. It must also be clean and be free of excessive bruising.

· STORAGE ·

Rather than letting gluts of fruit, vegetables, flowers or herbs go to waste, they can be stored and converted into syrup or wine at a more convenient time.

Above: Small leaved-herbs are prepared for drying.
Below: Herbs hanging up to dry in a warm room.

• Fruits

Some fruits, such as apples, store well. Do not attempt to store early varieties. Mid-season varieties will last three to four weeks in a draught-free place. Late keeping sorts store well.

Sort the apples roughly into size and store them in separate containers. Large fruits do not store for as long as the smaller ones. Do not attempt to store any that are bruised or scabbed or have no stalks.

Successful storage requires a temperature of 4.5°C/40°F in a draught-free, fairly moist situation (to delay shrivelling), in the dark or semi-dark and away from strong smells. Before storing, cool the fruit by keeping outside overnight. Fill a polythene bag, any size and of medium thickness, carefully with fruit, fold back the mouth of the bag and place the bag so that the fold is underneath. Maintain at an even temperature of 4.5°C/40°F (or a little under). Examine the bags periodically and discard any where rotting is occurring through condensation.

Pears should be picked whilst still hard and green. They may be stored unwrapped, laid out singly for ease of checking, since ripening happens very quickly.

Green tomatoes ripen slowly in the dark when cool. They soon turn red when brought into the warmth and light.

• Vegetables

Green leafy vegetables should never be stored. Root crops such as beetroots, parsnips, carrots and turnips should be lifted as dry as possible. Twist off their green tops and carefully brush off any soil adhering to the roots. Pack sound specimens in boxes of dry sand and store in a shed or cellar. Root crops can also be left in the ground. Mark the rows well so that they can be found easily when the tops have died down.

Cut marrows, pumpkins leaving 5 cm/2 in. of stem attached. Hang in nets in a cool, dry, frost proof store.

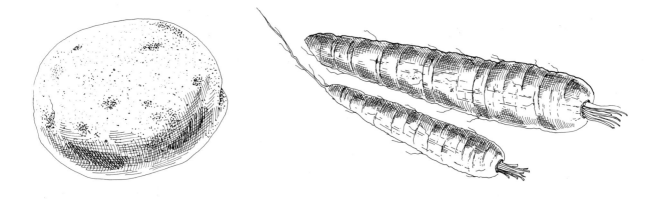

• DRYING •

Fruit (apples, pears, plums, damsons) Use clean, slatted wooden trays or stretch wire netting or thin, knitted cotton cloth or muslin (pre-washed and dried) on a framework of slats. Clean apples and pears should be peeled, cored and cut into rings. Stoned fruit should be washed and dried. Lay the fruit on the trays and dry at 50–65°C/120–150°F. Allow the dried fruit to cool overnight at room temperature, then pack in airtight boxes lined with kitchen paper. The browning of apple and pear rings can be prevented by pre-soaking in a salt solution (60 g/2 oz per 5 litres/1 gallon) for 10 minutes. Drain and dab dry before putting in the oven.

Herbs are best used fresh but commercially dried herbs are very good, especially if stored correctly. In the home, with only simple equipment, the choice of herbs for drying is more restricted.

Aromatic herbs, such as thyme, rosemary and sage dry well. Parsley, marjoram, basil and balm can be dried and, although the flavour is different from fresh, they can still be used. Herbs such as chervil, mint and dill are best frozen.

Gather stems of woody herbs by cutting back to the previous year's growth at the young leaf stage and before flowering begins. Soft-stemmed herbs can be cut to the ground. Gather flower heads in full bloom and seeds when the pods ripen and turn yellow or brown. Always gather after the dew has evaporated and before the sun gets hot.

Bunches of small leaved herbs can be tied, covered loosely with muslin and left hanging upside down from the ceiling of a warm room. Pick the leaves from large leaved herbs and dry on kitchen paper on trays either in the air or in a cool oven at 45–55°C/110–130°F for one hour. Dry until crisp, crush, remove any stems and pack into airtight jars; store in the dark.

The colour of parsley can be preserved by first dipping the leaves in boiling water for one minute, then for the same time in cold water. Shake the heads and press between kitchen paper. Dry in an oven at 115°C/240°F for an hour, turn off the heat and leave in the cooling oven until quite crisp.

Herbs can also be dried in a microwave oven. Spread them on kitchen paper and heat at full power for 1–2 minutes, depending on the amount of material. Stir occasionally. This is the best method for preserving colour.

Seed heads and pods can be dried in a cool oven (45–55°C/110–130°F) after enclosing in loosely tied paper bags (in case seeds fall out of the pods). Alternatively, place on cloth covered trays and leave for about a week in a warm room turning daily. The seeds drop out when the dried heads or pod are rubbed between the hands.

Flowers for drying should be picked early in the morning. Petals of flowers with prominent calyces such as the dandelion and primrose should be snipped off with scissors as soon as they are picked. They will be difficult to separate after drying. Lay the flowers or petals in a single layer on a clean cloth and leave in a dry, shady place. A low oven heat (45–55°C/110–130°F) may also be used but the colours suffer.

Flowers can also be dried in a microwave oven. Spread them on kitchen paper and use the defrost setting for four to five minutes. The natural colour is preserved.

• FREEZING •

Fruit Most types of fruit freeze well for use later in wine-making. Select sound specimens, prepare, bag, seal and freeze quickly.

Remove the stalks of berries and blackcurrants before freezing. Caster sugar can be added in the amount recommended in the wine-making recipe, simplifying subsequent juice and wine-making. Fruits that darken when cut (apples, pears, peaches, nectarines and white cherries) should be dusted with vitamin C powder at the rate of 2 g/5 kg or ½ tsp/10 lb, to inactivate the oxidising enzymes. Soft fruits can also be puréed in a food processor, preferably with vitamin C, before bagging, sealing and freezing. Small varieties of tomatoes, whole or as purées, can be frozen. Remove frozen fruit for juice and wine-making from the bags and leave to thaw overnight. The fruit can then be crushed easily, a pectolytic enzyme added and the juice squeezed out when the pectin test is negative (page 151).

Herbs can be frozen when young. Blanch as described for parsley (page 19) prior to drying, drain, freeze and seal in freezer bags, foil parcels or in water in the ice cube tray. When required, chop while frozen or use the cubes directly.

• CHEMICAL PRESERVATION •

Fruit Whole stone fruits (plums, damsons etc.) can be preserved chemically by complete immersion in a solution made up from one Campden tablet per 300 ml/½ pint water per 500 g/1 lb of fruit. Peel, core and slice apples before immersion. Seal the preserving jars.

When required, pour the complete contents of the jar(s) into a preserving pan and simmer gently until there is no further smell of sulphur dioxide. When cool, treat with a pectic enzyme and squeeze out the juice when the pectin test is negative (page 151).

Do not discard the liquid in which the fruit was stored, use the same volume as given for water in the wine-making recipe. Note that coloured fruits are bleached by the treatment, but the colour is restored during the boiling. Juices from fruit preserved in this way need an extra 3 mg Benerva (vitamin B₁) tablet per 5 litres/1 gallon to the amount given in the recipe when making wine.

• Commercial Products

Canned or bottled fruits and pulps; bottles, cans or cartons of a wide range of fruit juices; cans or cartons of concentrated juices (including those blended especially for wine-making); dried fruits, flowers, herbs, grains and spices can all be used. If not packaged exclusively for home wine-making, check the list of ingredients for freedom from the following preservatives: E200–203, E210–219, E220–227. These could delay the onset or rate of fermentation. Some of the products, such as concentrated grape juice, raisins and sultanas can be used in conjuction with freshly gathered raw materials.

• Water

Water for wine-making should be of normal drinking water quality. Excess chlorine is counteracted by adding an extra half Campden tablet per 5 litres/1 gallon to the number given in the recipe, or by boiling and cooling before use. Water with a high content of colouring matter, derived from peaty soils, is not desirable. Very hard water is better pre-boiled, cooled and filtered before use, especially when using fruits high in pectin.

• Sugar

The raw material should impart a pleasant flavour to the final wine. The amount of sugar present in any raw material grown is usually ignored since it will be insufficient to give the amount of alcohol required in the wine. Some fruits are so acid (blackcurrant) or so astringent (elderberry) that a degree of dilution is necessary to obtain a good flavour balance. For these reasons, sugar must be added before fermentation.

When making sugar additions, distinction must always be made between *adding to* 5 litres or 1 gallon or making up to those total volumes. In the first case the final volume is increased by 315 ml/10 fl oz for every 500 g/l lb added. The second method is used in this book.

The amount of sugar required will depend on the final alcohol content needed in the wine. A dry wine should contain 12 per cent alcohol and a sweet wine 15 per cent. These levels will be given by the complete fermentation of the following amounts of sugar.

	For a final volume of:	
	Five Litres	**One Gallon**
Dry wines (12 % alcohol)	1,125 g	2 lb 4 oz
Sweet wines (15 % alcohol)	1,375 g	2 lb 12 oz

Sugar can also be used for sweetening a dry wine. The corresponding weights of sugar for the required specific gravity can be found from the following table (the potential alcohol contents shown are only very approximate). If the gravity of the dry wine is less than 1.000, either increase the specific gravity by a number of degrees or to a particular value. For example, a wine of specific gravity 995 raised 10°, would have a final gravity of 1.005 but would need a 15° rise to achieve specific gravity 1.010. The amounts of sugar in the recipes have been calculated to produce alcohol contents and sweetnesses appropriate to the different types of wine.

Where honey, containing 75 per cent sugar, is specified, the amounts to be used will be greater than when using white sugar. The dry wines shown above would need 1½ kg/3 lb of honey instead of 1⅛ kg/2¼ lb of white sugar. Similar adjustments are needed for dried fruits, concentrated juices and other white sugar substitutes, according to their sugar contents.

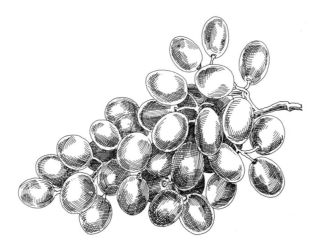

• Specific gravity and the corresponding weights of white sugar (sucrose)

Specific gravity	Approximate *potential* alcohol	Amount of sugar added and the volume *made up* to:		
	% volume	5 litres gram	1 gallon lb	oz
1.005	0.2	65		2
1.010	0.9	130		$4\frac{1}{4}$
1.015	1.6	195		$6\frac{1}{4}$
1.020	2.3	260		$8\frac{1}{4}$
1.025	3.0	325		$10\frac{1}{2}$
1.030	3.7	390		$12\frac{1}{2}$
1.035	4.4	455		$14\frac{1}{2}$
1.040	5.1	520	1	$0\frac{1}{2}$
1.045	5.8	585	1	$2\frac{3}{4}$
1.050	6.5	650	1	$4\frac{3}{4}$
1.055	7.2	715	1	7
1.060	7.85	780	1	9
1.065	8.6	850	1	$11\frac{1}{4}$
1.070	9.25	915	1	$13\frac{1}{4}$
1.075	9.95	980	1	$15\frac{1}{2}$
1.080	10.6	1,045	2	$1\frac{1}{2}$
1.085	11.3	1,110	2	$3\frac{1}{2}$
1.090	12.0	1,175	2	$5\frac{1}{2}$
1.095	12.7	1,245	2	$7\frac{3}{4}$
1.100	13.45	1,310	2	10
1.105	14.15	1,375	2	12
1.110	14.9	1,440	2	14
1.115	15.6	1,495	3	0

SPECIALISED WINE-MAKING INGREDIENTS

Wine can be made from fruits, sugar, water and yeast only, but unless it is quite acid, spoilage organisms and oxidative enzyme changes would be uncontrolled. The wine could be variable in flavour, even hazy, hence the ancient practice of adding brandy to stabilise such wines before they were fully fermented.

Good, clear wines can now be made consistently, without adding brandy. The ingredients used in place of brandy are described below and their use is specified in the recipe chapters.

• Sulphur Dioxide (SO$_2$)

Usually sold in the form of Campden tablets which, when added to an acid solution, releases sulphur dioxide, a powerful bactericide. One tablet is added per 5 litres/1 gallon. Unlike the SO$_2$ sterilising solution (page 14), the amount of SO$_2$ in juices and extracts are too small to be perceptible on the nose.

The more acid the solution (or, more accurately, the lower the pH) the more effective is the same dose of SO$_2$. It has three main functions:
(a) destroys spoilage organisms that require air for growth;
(b) inhibits enzymatic oxidation (i.e. prevents cut fruits from browning);
(c) combines with oxygen in a bottled wine, keeping it fresh in flavour for a longer period.

• Yeast Nutrients

Yeast needs nutrients to remain active and without a good supply it dies and ceases to ferment. Many fruits, some vegetables and grains contain sufficient nutrients, but other raw materials such as flowers and herbs have very little.

The following nutrients are available: simple ammonium salts; these plus B group vitamins or plus amino acids and vitamins; or yeast autolysate. Use as directed on the label. Otherwise add the following two ingredients when yeast nutrients are specified in the recipe.

(a) BP quality ammonium sulphate or diammonium phosphate, using $2\frac{1}{2}$–5 g/$\frac{1}{2}$ tsp per 5 litres/1 gallon or $\frac{1}{2}$ tsp of each for the same volume *and*

(b) Thiamin hydrochloride or vitamin B$_1$ at the rate of 3 mg per 5 litres/ 1 gallon. It is also sold by chemists under the trade name Benerva in 3 mg tablets. Larger sized tablets are available if greater quantities of raw material are to be processed consistently.

• Acids

Acids are required not only for the yeast, but also to improve colour extraction from red raw materials and enhance the bouquet and flavour of the wine. Yeast can only function efficiently in a mildly acid solution. The three acids most commonly used are citric, malic and tartaric. Use as directed in the recipes. Sometimes lemon or orange juice or cream of tartar is specified for the same purpose.

• Enzymes

Pectic enzyme is used when making wine from fruit to dissolve the natural pectin content. It also helps to extract all the juice and flavour as well as preventing a pectin haze in the finished wine. Hot water extraction also extracts soluble pectin.

Rohament P is an enzyme which releases the individual cells of the viscous pulp from highly pectinous fruits (e.g. blackcurrants). It is used either to treat pulp before it is pressed to make nectars, or is used in conjunction with a pectin enzyme to remove all pectin quickly; the juice can then be removed quite easily by squeezing the treated pulp in a closely woven cloth.

Protein enzyme Some fruits, such as white grapes, contain small amounts of soluble protein that causes a haze when wine made from it is chilled. Treatment of the extract with a protein enzyme (or fining with Bentonite, page 26) removes the problem.

Starch enzyme Preparing an extract by boiling young vegetables or cereals extracts soluble starch, another cause of haze. A starch destroying enzyme is now available for adding to the warm extract. It is sometimes sold as a mixture with a protein enzyme.

• Fining Agents

Few wines need fining since most of them clear naturally. If a faint haze does remain however allow the wine to resettle before fining the syphoned off wine. Directions for using fining agents are given in Problems of Wine-Making (page 148).

Gelatin Dissolve 5 g/½ oz BP quality tannic acid in 100 ml/½ pint water *and* dissolve 5 g/½ oz edible grade gelatin (leaf or powder) in 100 ml/½ pint boiling water stirring vigorously until completely dissolved.

The stock solutions do not keep well, so make them up when several hazy wines need treating.

Bentonite A natural, pure dry clay. Make a 5 per cent suspension (5 g/100 ml or 1 oz/1 pint) at least 24 hours before required, using one of the three following methods. Once made the suspension lasts almost indefinitely. It is possible to buy the suspension already made.
(a) Put the ingredients in a blender or liquidiser and leave it running for a few minutes. Repeat, if necessary *or*
(b) Mix the powder into a stiff paste with some of the water. Add further quantities of water, mixing thoroughly after each addition, until a uniform suspension is obtained *or*
(c) Put the ingredients in a saucepan or beaker and stir vigorously while heating to 50°C/120°F. Repeat the treatment for the next 2 days.

Chitin Derived from the shells of shrimps and crabs. It is very effective against a number of hazes. Use as directed by the manufacturer.

Isinglass Pure protein made from the swim bladder of the sturgeon; use as directed.

JUICE EXTRACTION
& TREATMENT

· EXTRACTION ·

The method required for extracting the juices, colour and flavouring matter from the raw material will depend on its composition. There are four main methods of juice extraction: direct pressing; cold water or wine extraction; pulp fermentation and hot water extraction or boiling. Wine-makers starting with commercial, single strength or concentrated juices can ignore this chapter, since no extraction is involved, other than the addition of water to the concentrate.

· Directing Pressing

Juice from grapes can be extracted directly by squeezing the berries in a press. Except for red-fleshed varieties, both red and white grapes give a white juice. Better yields are obtained by crushing before pressing. Apples and pears must be crushed before pressing.

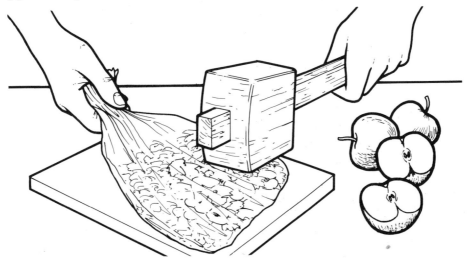

Apples must be crushed before pressing. Place a few at a time in a plastic bag and then crush with a mallet.

Screw down the pressure plate until
the flow stops then remove the
straining bag, stir up the pulp within
and press again.

Juice yields can be improved by pre-treating the pulp with a pectic
enzyme (see the manufacturer's instructions). Most berries and
currants are so rich in pectin that the pulp is viscous and *must* be
warmed and enzymed. The process is speeded up by stirring and
adding Rohament-P (page 25). After the combined treatments, the
juice can be squeezed out quite easily in a thick woven cloth or in a
press.

• Cold Extraction

Some materials, such as flowers and herbs have no 'juice' to release on
pressing. Flavour is extracted by steeping either in cold water or a

For flower wines, rub the steeping petals against
the side of the bowl with a wooden spoon to
extract the flavouring essences.

sugar solution. It is also usual to add three Campden tablets and 5–10 g/$\frac{1}{6}$–$\frac{1}{3}$ oz acid per 5 litres/1 gallon to prevent microbial spoilage and enzymic oxidation.

If a press is not available even relatively juicy fruits such as apples and pears can be treated in this way. Thinly slice and steep in water to which a pectic enzyme and two Campden tablets have been added per 5 litres/1 gallon. When the slices become transparent they should be squeezed out in a strong, woven cloth and the liquid added to the extraction liquid which is then sweetened and yeasted. Neutral flavoured, white wine is very effective as an extractant and can produce a reasonable wine quickly for early drinking.

• Pulp Fermentation

It is traditional to ferment red grapes 'on the skins'. The pulp (often after removal of the stalks) is mixed with a little sulphur dioxide (1 Campden tablet per 5 kg/10 lb) and left for 1–3 days depending on the grape variety. The yeast is usually added about six hours after sulphiting.

The pulp tends to rise above the juice and has to be resubmerged at intervals to improve the colour development. Red grapes give red juice as the extractants are sulphur dioxide and the alcohol and carbon dioxide produced during fermentation.

Even the cold extraction process can be speeded up by adding sugar and yeast about six hours after sulphiting. The extracted material is strained off as before, and fermentation continues in the liquid.

When fermenting on the pulp, the fruit can be pressed down under the surface of the liquid by weighing it down with a sterilised china plate.

• Hot Extraction

Cells of fruits and vegetables break down when heated, releasing juice or flavouring the extracting water. Several methods are possible:

(a) Bring the cleaned and chopped vegetables and water to the boil and simmer until *just* tender. Remove from the heat and strain. Acid is usually added with the water for a better colour. Any spices (crushed not powdered) can be placed in a muslin bag suspended in the boiling water. Some berry fruits and currants are placed with a little water in a double saucepan with the outer jacket heated to 70°C/160°F, until the juice flows freely. The residue is then strained off.

(b) Cover destoned and halved plums, damsons, peaches, with boiling water. When the liquid reaches 40°C/105°F, add two Campden tablets per 5 litres/1 gallon and pectic enzyme. Leave for 1–2 days or until the residue can be squeezed out easily in a cloth. Crushed cereals are also steeped but without the enzyme.

(c) Place the clean, roughly chopped material in a steam extractor, heat the boiler and collect the clear, virtually sterile juice that runs out.

Extracts made by heating may contain some pectin, and should be treated with a pectic enzyme routinely. If the wine is still hazy after fermentation, test for protein and/or starch (Problems of Wine-Making page 148).

• TREATMENT •

The raw materials for wine-making contain not only juice and colouring agents but also moulds, yeasts, bacteria and the nutrients on which these feed. Oxidising enzymes are also present which, if not inhibited, would produce an unpleasant dark wine.

It is possible to destroy both the unwanted organisms and enzymes by boiling the pulp and extract, but unless this is carried out carefully, it could cause protein and pectin hazes in the wine. For this reason, the unwanted organisms are destroyed by treating with sulphur dioxide.

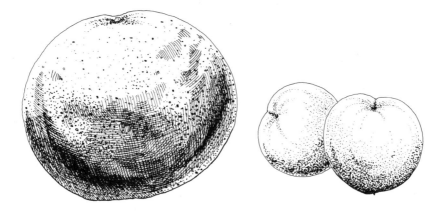

◆ Sulphiting

The amount of sulphur dioxide required will depend on the acidity of the juice. In general the following amounts of sulphur dioxide are needed when using good quality raw materials:

Acidity	Parts per million of SO_2	Campden tablets per 5 litres/1 gallon
Very acid (Bramley's Seedling apples)	75	1.5
Moderate (Dessert apples, plums)	120	2.5
Low	150–200	3–4

Rather than using high levels of SO_2 in low acid juices or extracts, it is better to add 10 g/⅓ oz per 5 litres/1 gallon citric or malic acid and 2–3 Campden tablets, or the juice of a lemon or two limes.

There is always a bleaching effect when coloured juices are sulphited. The colour returns during the subsequent yeast fermentation.

A delay or 6–24 hours is advocated between sulphiting and yeasting otherwise the SO_2 would react with the yeast as well as destroying unwanted enzymes, moulds and bacteria, and so delay the start of fermentation.

Other additions to the juice are sugar to produce the required alcohol content and any yeast nutrients, should the extract have insufficient. Some home wine-makers add them routinely to ensure consistent, rapid fermentation.

YEAST CULTURES
& FERMENTATION

• YEAST CULTURES •

Most wine-makers use commercial preparations of wine yeast which are sold as tablets, granules, powder or liquid preparations. All of these are readily available. It is obvious which yeast should be used for champagne and sherry. The choice of yeast for non-specialised wine is not as obvious. A Sauterne yeast will not automatically make a Sauterne wine, nor a Chablis yeast a Chablis. To produce the characteristics of such wines particular raw materials and methods are necessary. The normal yeast for most wines should be capable of readily producing the amount of alcohol required, the nutrient requirements should not to be too specialised and the yeast should settle out readily at the end of fermentation, forming a firm deposit and not producing unpleasant taints. It is better to start with a general purpose yeast culture and see how it behaves for different types of wines.

For interest, a double quantity of a sweetened juice or extract can be divided into two and the two parts fermented with different yeast cultures. In this way experience with different yeasts can be gathered under actual making conditions.

• Amount to Use

The amount of yeast to use will be given on the packet. A dry yeast should be stirred into about 150 ml/$\frac{1}{4}$ pint of luke warm water (30°C/85°F) and left about two hours before using. (A sterilised wine bottle can be used for this purpose.) This re-hydrates the yeast cells so that growth can start sooner in the sweetened extract.

The metric measurement for fermentation in this book is five litres. There will be a surplus of yeasted juice or extract when a one gallon (5 litre) jar is filled. The surplus should be put into a bottle fitted with an air-lock. It can be used for topping up the main bulk during fermentation, and when the contents of the jar are fermented and racked, any shortage in the storage jar, can be made up with wine racked from the bottle.

Above: Root crops can be stored in boxes of dry sand.
Below: Specialised ingredients ensure that good clear wines can be made consistently.

A sterilised wine bottle can be used to prepare a yeast starter.

• FERMENTATION •

Fermentation is the process in which sugar is converted to alcohol by the enzymes secreted in the yeast cells. It can be conducted 'on the pulp', i.e. in the presence of solids in a bin, or in a fermentation jar sealed with an air-lock. Fermentation begins as soon as the yeast starts working and continues until it stops (this can be because it has converted all the sugar to alcohol and carbon dioxide or that is has produced so much alcohol it can tolerate no more).

The addition of sulphur dioxide to a sweetened juice is followed by a rapid fall in numbers of 'wild' organisms present. After some six hours, more than 90 per cent of these will have been destroyed. Most of the rest die over the next 18 hours. It is then safe to add the rehydrated fermenting yeast.

When the yeast is added it begins to reproduce itself, living on the

Juice is obtained by direct pressing immediately after crushing the apples.

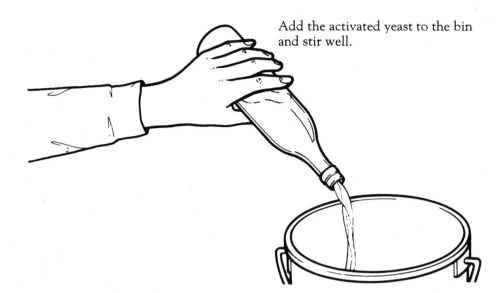

Add the activated yeast to the bin and stir well.

sugar to sustain and nourish each of the millions of new cells formed. In doing this it produces as by-products alcohol and carbon dioxide. Fusel oils and organic acids are also produced. The exact amounts are determined by the type of yeast used, the temperature and conditions of fermentation. Lack of some nutrients can adversely affect the acidity of the wine, or the speed of fermentation, which is another reason why nutrients are added, especially to low nutrient juices.

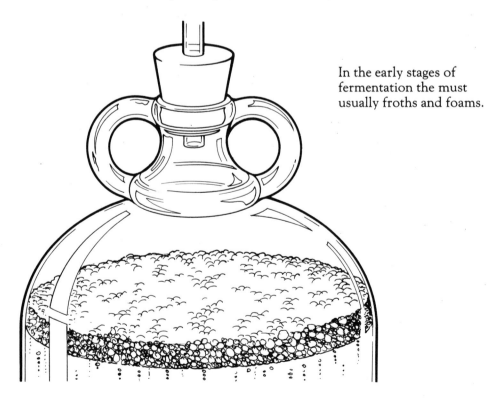

In the early stages of fermentation the must usually froths and foams.

• Froth Formation

Fermentation produces bubbles of carbon dioxide which rise in the liquid and with some of the yeast cells form a head. The first fermentation is normally carried out in an open-mouthed vessel covered with cling film or a clean cloth. When froth formation has ceased, the liquid is strained and then poured back into the fermentation vessel. The contents are made up to volume with water (or wine from the spare bottle) and the air-lock fitted.

After fermenting on the pulp, the solid matter is strained off and discarded, and the liquid is then put into a sterilised fermentation vessel.

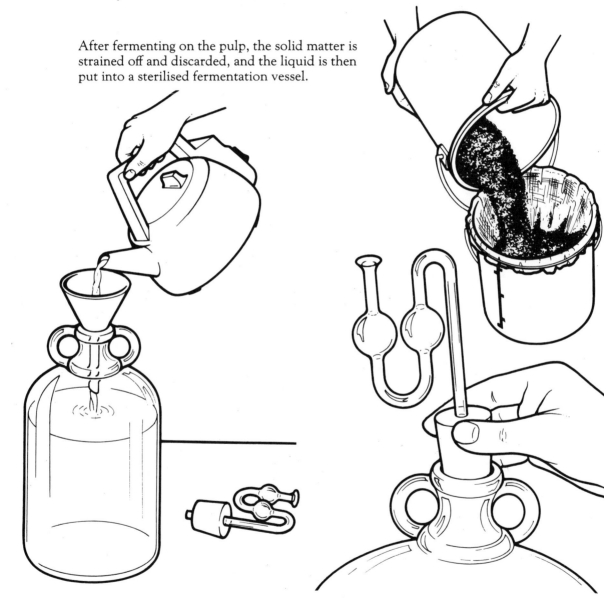

Top up the must with tap water or cold boiled water if it is hard or excessively chlorinated.

The air-lock and bung are placed in the neck of the fermentation vessel.

In the early stages of fermentation bubbles of gas hurry through the air-lock.

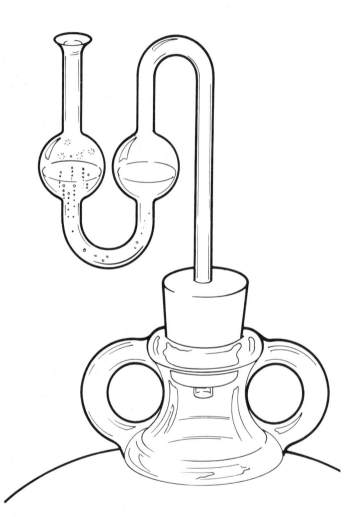

When fermentation finishes, the wine starts to clear and a heavy sediment can be seen at the bottom of the jar.

• Remainder of Fermentation

The period of fermentation may vary from two weeks to several months, depending on the yeast, composition of the extract and its temperature. When gas bubbles cease to form, the wine should be tasted. If it is dry or has reached the required degree of sweetness, remove the jars to a cool place for a specified length of time. If you are not happy with the colour, flavour or degree of dryness there are several steps you can take (Problems of Wine-Making page 148).

Ferment in a warm place, or in cold weather use a heated pad, to maintain an even temperature.

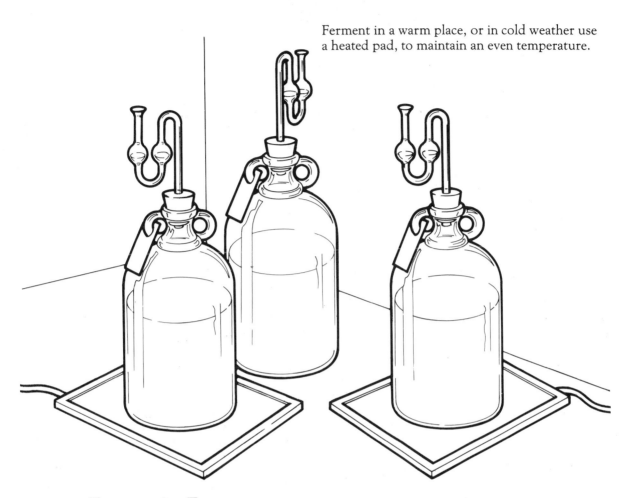

• **Fermentation Temperatures**

The working temperature limits for fermentation are 15–25°C/60–75°F, depending on the type of wine being made. However, if the room in which the fermentation takes place is much colder or warmer, or if the temperature fluctuates widely during each 24 hours, the yeast can be seriously affected and may become dormant or even die out prematurely (Problems of Wine-Making page 148). The bottom of the airing cupboard or a thermostatically controlled, electrical heating jacket or heating tray will help to regulate the temperature. *Never* keep wine that is fermenting in a glass jar in direct sunlight as it is liable to become overheated.

WINE TREATMENT

THE wine is stored for a time between the end of fermentation and bottling. This allows it to clear, prevents unwanted yeast fermentation later in the bottle and ensures it has an agreeable flavour balance.

Some two or three weeks after placing the fermented wine into cool storage, rack or syphon off the wine without disturbing the yeast deposit. Taste the wine. It will not necessarily be very attractive, often tasting a little thin and yeasty, but a sound wine improves enormously on storage. The object at this stage is to ensure it has no major flavour defects.

• Flavour Balance

Wine to be made sweet or sparkling will need other treatments (pages 45 and 48), but the following points are as relevant as they are for still, dry table wines.

All wines should be free of taints; see Problems of Wine-Making (page 148) for descriptions and treatment of such faults. Never blend a tainted wine with a sound one, the result is always disappointing. The particular qualities to look for in a sound wine are as follows:

A base wine to be rendered sparkling should be lightly brisk or acidic, fresh in flavour, without any marked taste except possibly lightly floral.

Base wines for finishing as dessert, social or country wines will already have a higher alcohol content than those for sparkling or table wines. They should be robust in flavour and even have marked taste characteristics (such as raisin, raspberry, elderberry etc.) although these will mellow with age.

Dry table wines should be fresh and clean and sufficiently acid, if white or rosé, to induce slight salivation. Reds can vary from fresh easy drinking wines to those needing storage for mellowing. Hence the latter can be a little astringent and even purple in colour when young.

With experience it is possible to predict how the wines will taste after storage, especially if the suggestions for tasting commercial wines (page 55) are followed.

(a)

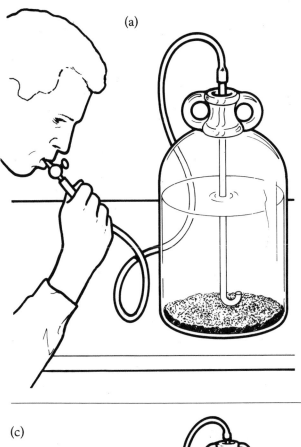

(b)

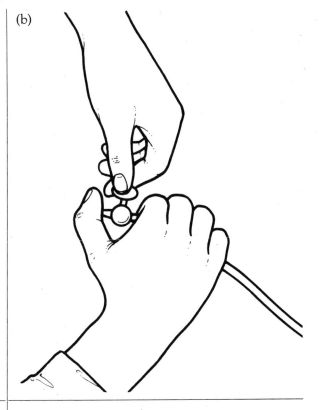

(c)

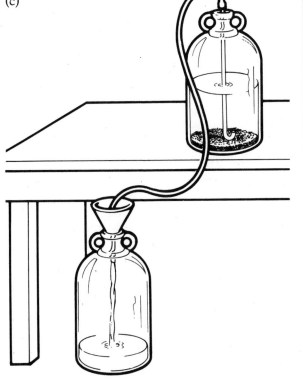

(a) To rack the finished wine into a clean, sterilised demijohn, insert a syphon and j-tube into the jar which is full, and suck the other end of the syphon until the wine starts to flow.

(b) Close the valve on the plastic tap (or pinch the tube firmly between the finger and thumb if not using a tap).

(c) Insert the end of the tube into the empty demijohn, placed *below* the full demijohn and open the plastic tap. Racking is complete when only the sediment remains in the higher demijohn.

• Correcting Flavour Imbalance

Some correction of flavour imbalance is possible at this stage. When several wines are available in vessels or jars, taste and record their flavours. Looking carefully at the notes afterwards may show that an excess (e.g. of acidity) in one could be counterbalanced by a deficiency in the same characteristics in another. Or, lack of depth may need correcting by, say, mixing raisin wine with elderflower wine.

Make trial blends using *measured* small quantities. Correct if necessary. This is not a process to be hurried and better carried out over several short sessions, so that the palate (and the taster) does not get fatigued.

Make up the blend(s) on the larger scale and continue as for Still, Dry Wines (pages 38–44). Blended wines may re-ferment for a short time, but they are perfectly safe kept under a storage bung.

If suitable wines are not available for blending, some correction of flavour imbalance is still possible at this stage. If the wine is *too sour* (not vinegary) due to the raw materials being more acid than allowed for in the recipes, it can be ameliorated by diluting with a proportion of sweetened water (1½ kg/3 lb sugar per 5 litres/1 gallon of water), yeasting and re-fermenting. This is to prevent unnecessary dilution of the alcohol content. Do not dilute excessively or the final wine will be insipid. When fully re-fermented, cool and store for two to three weeks as before.

Excess bitterness can be treated in a similar manner (but not if too many elderberry stalks were mixed in with the fruit originally).

Excessively sweet wines need blending with dry wines of a similar character, or add 10 per cent of water, or return to the warmth in an attempt to ferment away some of the excess (see also the treatment of stuck fermentations page 148).

Lack of 'body' or depth of flavour can be compensated for by adding about 245 g/8½ oz of grape concentrate to 5 litres/1 gallon of fermented wine and re-fermenting. The addition of mashed raisins or sultanas (250 g/½ lb per 5 litres/1 gallon) serves the same purpose.

Lack of aroma of the raw material especially of flowers, can be corrected by infusing more of the same material in the stored wine. Use fresh flower or herb material, when available or the dried article, but for the last only use a minimum of 30 g/1 oz per 5 litres/1 gallon.

• WINE TYPES •

• Still, dry table wines

Once the desired flavour balance has been produced it is necessary to minimise exposure of the wine to air. Hence add 1 Campden tablet per 5 litres/1 gallon. Fill the storage jar completely and seal, preferably with a safety bung. Store in a cool place for three months. This is necessary for the flavour to improve, to allow the wine to clear naturally, to ensure there is a minimum of live yeast cells and, for dry wines no residual sugar (see page 50 for a simple sugar test) to cause re-fermentation in bottle.

Some wines containing malic acid, whether present naturally (from apples, pears, grapes) or added, can undergo another type of fermentation, called malo-lactic, but it is rare in home-made wines. Any lactic acid bacteria, derived originally from the fruit and only inhibited temporarily by sulphiting and yeast fermentation, start to grow when the temperature of the stored wine rises above 15°C/60°F. Malic acid is converted to lactic acid and carbon dioxide. The amount of gas is much less than from the yeast fermentation of sugar. If it occurs in the bottle, the wine becomes lightly carbonated but the bottles do not burst.

The jars are stored for at least three months and examined again. If the recipe has been followed properly, the wine should have clarified satisfactorily. Clearing starts from the top of the jar and, in a steady cool temperature, proceeds downwards until a firm deposit has formed. If a jar has not cleared satisfactorily, then carry out the diagnostic tests given in Problems of Wine-Making (page 148). Or add a commercial wine fining, starting with one based on chitin, as this is effective against several types of haze (page 26).

Light wines can be bottled after three months' storage if they are clear and have shown no signs of yeast fermentation. Full-bodied wines would benefit from another three months' storage.

Whenever bottling is contemplated, taste the wine again to ensure it is satisfactory. Syphon it into a jar or bin without disturbing any deposit. Ensure the outlet of the syphon reaches the bottom of the receiving vessel (preferably one fitted with a tap at the base) to avoid excessive aeration. Dissolve one Campden tablet in each 5 litres/1 gallon of the wine and stir gently. If the wines are to be entered in competitions, they should be fined and/or filtered before bottling.

When fermentation is quite finished, syphon the clear wine into bottles.

Fill clear table-wine bottles from the tap or a second syphon, without splashing. Red wines are put into dark bottles, unless they are to be entered in competitions, in which case use the clear bottles specified (and store in the dark).

Insert a pre-soaked, new bark cork or a plastic stopper, and drive in hard. Wipe the top of the cork and, if bark corks have been used, leave standing upright for at least 24 hours to allow the corks to swell.

Keep bottles of the same wine together in a suitably labelled carton

Insert corks using (a) a mallet *or* (b) a corking machine, then label each bottle and store in a cool place while the wine matures.

or box. It is probably better to label just before the wine is ready for drinking.

Finally, the bottles should be kept on their sides in a cool, dark cupboard (or preferably in a cellar) at least another month for the flavours to 'marry' together. Except for low alcohol wines (e.g. rosés), longer storage will give further improvement, if patience allows. A good wine will last some years if it has been made properly, kept well corked and cool. Storage can never improve an ill-favoured or tainted wine.

· SUMMARY OF METHOD FOR FINISHING ·
DRY, STILL WINES

At the end of each recipe for dry, table wines, the wine-maker is directed to this page for the final treatment. See pages 38–44 for any further details.

1. Move the fermentation vessel to a cool room or cupboard with the air-lock still in place.

2. Leave for 2–3 weeks.

3. Syphon off the wine, leaving the yeast deposit behind.

4. Blend or adjust the wine to give a good flavour balance and fill the storage jar.

5. Keep for 2–3 weeks in the warm under an air-lock in case of re-fermentation.

6. Return to cool storage, dissolve in one Campden tablet per 5 litres/ 1 gallon. Insert a storage bung.

7. Store cool, three months for a light wine, six months for a full-bodied wine.

8. Syphon off the wine, dissolve in one Campden tablet per 5 litres/ 1 gallon. Fine or filter, if necessary.

9. Bottle, cork, seal and store for at least another month.

· Sweet, Still Wines

After correcting any flavour imbalance, following the first racking after two to three weeks storage, it is necessary to sweeten the wine and stabilise it against re-fermentation in the bottle by any residual yeast. Several methods are used:

1. Dry wines can be sweetened to taste with non-fermentable glycerin, and/or a proprietary wine sweetener. Dissolve in a little hot water before adding to the wine *or*

2. The wine can be made more alcoholic by further fermentation(s) until it is no longer fermentable. Sugar is dissolved in the first racked dry wine at the rate of 250 g/½ lb per 5 litres/1 gallon. The air-lock is re-inserted and the jar returned to the warmth. Any further fermentation will be slow. When gas bubbles no longer form, taste the wine. If it is not sweet, make a further addition of sugar (250 g/½ lb) and again keep warm. Repeat, if necessary, until the sugar remains unfermented. Keep warm for a further month, then transfer to the cool cupboard and treat thereafter as for Still, Dry Table Wines (above) *or*

3. As in point 2 except that the wine is racked every two months, resweetening to taste each time as necessary. When the fermentation finally ceases, make any necessary adjustment to sweetness, rack and store as for Still, Dry Table Wines (above).

After at least three months, rack and clarify by fining (and filtration

Topping up the fermentation jar with
the sugar syrup.

if needed). In addition to the one Campden tablet per 5 litres/1 gallon,
also add 1 g potassium sorbate per 5 litres/1 gallon. Sorbate must never
be added during fermentation since, if any lactic acid bacteria are
present, it is broken down to another compound which gives a
geranium-like flavour to the wine *or*

4. Full-bodied, sweet wines, can be pasteurised as described for Fruit
Juices, Cordials & Syrups (page 141). Ensure there is sufficient space
under the cork to allow expansion of the wine during heating.

· SUMMARY OF METHOD FOR FINISHING ·
SWEET, STILL WINES

At the end of each recipe for sweet, still wines (social, dessert or
country), the wine-maker is directed to this page for the final treatment. See page 44 for any further details and for alternative methods.

1. Move the fermentation vessel to a cold room or cupboard with the air-lock still in place.
2. Leave for 2–3 weeks.
3. Syphon off the wine leaving the yeast deposit behind.
4. Dissolve 250 g/½ lb white sugar in 5 litres/1 gallon of the wine.
5. Blend or adjust the wine to give a good flavour balance and fill the storage jar.
6. Re-insert the air-lock and keep at fermentation temperature.
7. When the gas bubbles cease to form, sweeten to taste, re-insert the air-lock and return to the warmth.
8. If the wine re-ferments, repeat point 7. The wine is stable when it retains its sweetness, even after being kept warm for a month.
9. Transfer the vessel to a cool room or cupboard and leave for 2–3 weeks.
10. Syphon off the wine, leaving the yeast deposit behind.
11. Dissolve in one Campden tablet per 5 litres/1 gallon. Insert a storage bung.
12. Store cool, three months for a light wine, six months for a full-bodied wine.
13. Syphon off the wine, dissolve in one Campden tablet per 5 litres/ 1 gallon. Fine or filter if necessary.
14. Bottle, cork and seal and store for at least another month.

• Draught Wines

Some wine-makers like to keep wine on tap. The plastic pressure barrels fitted with a carbon dioxide injector are ideal for the purpose. The gaseous atmosphere over the wine prevents flavour loss by oxidation while on tap.

Less expensive are used 5 gallon collapsible plastic wine containers which are sold cheaply by wine retailers when empty. They have a collapsible plastic inner lining, fitted with a tap and held inside a cardboard outer case. As wine is drawn off, the inner lining collapses, so that air cannot enter. Smaller new refillable collapsible plastic containers, also fitted with a tap, are now on sale. Alternatively divide the finished wine between a half gallon glass jar and three one-litre bottles each with a replaceable stopper. When the bottles are empty they can be washed and filled from the jar. Thus the wine is exposed only minimally to the air.

• Records

Is is a good habit to keep records of each batch of wine, showing the ingredients and wine-making methods used. Add the time taken for fermentation and when it was stored, racked and bottled. Comments should be added to the appropriate page or card each time a wine is tasted. In this way any necessary improvements can be made in future or successes repeated.

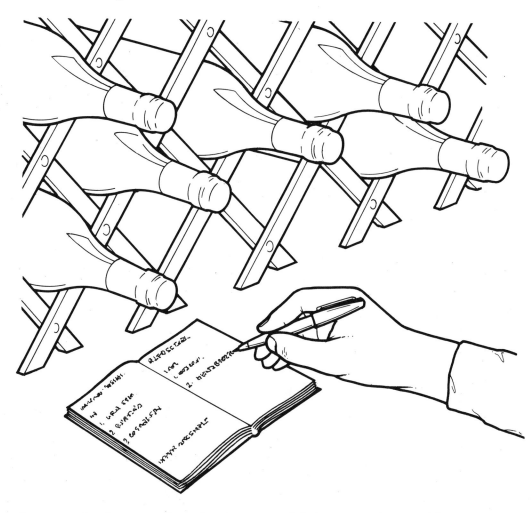

Store wine bottles in a rack, and make a note of their progress in a special record book.

SPARKLING
WINES

This is the most difficult type of wine to prepare as it is hard to strike a proper balance between the sugar content of the wine and the amount of carbon dioxide formed. Only the preparation of dry sparkling wines is described in this chapter. Any sweetening with sugar syrup should take place after disgorging (see page 51), and just before the wine is served.

A sparkling wine is made by slightly sweetening a base wine and allowing a secondary fermentation to take place in a sealed bottle. The carbon dioxide cannot escape and remains dissolved in the wine. The yeast deposit is removed and the bottle recorked after topping up. Further fermentation is prevented by the high gas pressure which, with the exhaustion of yeast nutrients, leads to the death of the yeast cells.

If the bottles are not new, they *must* have contained champagne previously. They are made of thick glass with sloping shoulders and a deep indentation or punt in the base. Ensure the empty bottles are free of flaws or cracks by inspecting them and lightly tapping them together.

· METHODS ·

The base wine should contain about 10 per cent alcohol, be fresh and clean on the palate, slightly acidic and not too strongly flavoured. It can be white, rosé or, occasionally, red. Recipes for base wines suitable for rendering sparkling are listed in the table at the end of this chapter. The base wine should contain no sugar. This can be checked by using the Clinitest (page 50) or the Test Bottling method opposite.

Empirical and controlled methods are available for making these wines. The results of the first may be a little erratic at times, but the method requires the minimum of effort.

Above: The different stages of fermentation show how wine develops from a cloudy to a crystal clear liquid.
Below: Keep records of each batch of wine so that improvements can be made in the future and successes repeated.

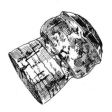

• Empirical Method

After the fermented wine has been kept for two or three weeks in a cool room or a refrigerator, it should be racked or syphoned off. If the wine is not reasonably clear, delay racking for another two weeks or fine lightly. Fill a champagne bottle with the wine and add two large raisins or sultanas, *or* one lump of sugar, *or* for each 5 litres/1 gallon of wine add 60 g/2 oz of sugar dissolved in 150 ml/¼ pint of water. Mix well and bottle. Tie or wire the corks down tightly and store the bottles on their sides in a cool room or cellar for six months. See Disgorging (page 51) for the remaining treatment.

• Test Bottling

Store the base wine in a number of small containers, or in a pressure cask. This will reduce any oxidation of the bulk of the wine during the tests, which should traditionally commence in February.

First dissolve 250 g/10 oz white sugar in 600 ml/1 pint water and measure 25 ml/1 fl oz into a half-size champagne bottle. Three-quarters fill the bottle with base wine and shake gently to mix. Cork, wire and keep in a warm cupboard. If, after two to three weeks the cork is seen to strain against the wire and there is a heavy yeast deposit, it is too soon to bottle the bulk. Empty the bottle into any batch of fermenting wine available.

Repeat the process at intervals until the cork strains a little against the wire, the deposit is small and the wine is reasonably carbonated when the bottle is opened. This indicates that there is just sufficient yeast and nutrients to carry out a safe bottle fermentation.

The bulk of the wine can now be sweetened with 125 ml/4 fl oz sugar syrup per 5 litres/1 gallon. Almost fill the bottles, cork, wire and store on their sides until adequately carbonated. *Either* move a bottle carefully to a refrigerator, without disturbing the yeast deposit, leave overnight and next day decant carefully into a jug before serving, *or*, use the disgorging procedure (page 51).

If the wine fails to ferment in the first test bottle, set up three more as follows. To the first add a little yeast nutrient, champagne yeast to the second and both to the third. Three-quarters fill each with the sweetened wine, cork, wire and keep warm. Treat the bulk as for the minimum treatment giving satisfactory carbonation.

When filtering wine it is important to place the wine that is to be filtered above the height of the receiving jar if a steady flow is to be maintained.

• Controlled Method

The base wine is first tested for sugar content, since this regulates the amount and hence pressure of gas produced. Chemists sell a home-kit for diabetics under the name Clinitest. Complete instructions are given on the package (no scientific knowledge is required).

With the dropper provided, place five drops of wine, ten of water and one of the tablets in the small test tube. A colour change takes place which, compared with the colour chart, gives the sugar content of the wine. If the Clinitest registers 0.2 per cent or less, the sugar content of the wine can be ignored and 60 g/2 oz sugar are then dissolved in 5 litres/1 gallon of the wine.

If the natural sugar content is more than 0.2 per cent, it must be deducted from the amount of sugar necessary to give the required degree of carbonation (1.3 per cent). Thus, subtract the sugar content (x) from 1.3 and then multiply by 50 for g/5 litres or by 1.6 for oz/1 gallon.

i.e. $(1.3 - x) \times 50 = $ g/5 litres
$(1.3 - x) \times 1.6 = $ oz/1 gallon

The answer must not be greater than 65 g/2 oz per 5 litres/1 gallon. Dissolve the calculated amount of sugar in the wine.

Using the amount specified on the packet, stir a dried champagne yeast in a little water at 30°C/85°F and leave for an hour to rehydrate. Now add one third of a Benerva tablet and a pinch (100 mg) of BP quality ammonium sulphate per 5 litres/1 gallon.

Stir the mixture vigorously to dissolve in a little oxygen for yeast growth and to distribute the yeast uniformly. Pour sufficient into a jar to fill a champagne bottle, leaving sufficient space to insert the stopper. Repeat for each bottle so they all have approximately the same amount of yeast. Moisten the hollow plastic stopper in water, drive in and wire or tie down. Store the bottles on their sides at 10–15°C/50–60°F.

• Disgorging

The yeast will start to grow by producing a white growth on the lower inner walls of the bottles. The wine slowly matures in flavour and after six months the yeast starts to die. Ideally the bottles should be left for a year if the full disgorging treatment, re-sweetening and bottling procedure is carried out.

However, there is a short cut which is less time consuming. Once the yeast deposit has formed, invert the bottles into a crate or carton with sub-divisions. By giving the bottles a twirl at intervals, the deposit is dislodged from the walls and falls into the hollow centre of the stopper.

When all the deposit is inside the stopper, the wine is ready for drinking. Take an inverted bottle outside. Cut the wire or tie while the neck of the bottle is held in the left hand (for right-handed wine-makers). The thumb of the left hand then eases out the stopper and is then pressed firmly and swiftly over the open end. Be ready in case the stopper flies out of its own accord as soon as the wire or tie is cut! With practice very little wine need be lost. Bring the bottle upright, insert a clean stopper or patent reclosure and place in a refrigerator for about one hour before serving. The wine can be sweetened safely just before serving by adding a small quantity of cold sugar syrup to taste.

• Recipes

The following recipes, given in the later chapters, are suitable for making the base wine. However, use 1 kg/2 lb white sugar per 5 litres/ 1 gallon, instead of the amount specified in the original recipe. Once the base wine is made use either of the above methods to make it sparkling.

	Red	*White/Fawn*	*Rosé*
Fruit Wines	Bilberry 1, 2 Blackcurrant 1 (variation 1) Cherry 2 Damson 2 and (variation 2) Gooseberry 1 and (variations 1 and 5)	Apple 2 (variations 1 and 2) Apple 3 Gooseberry 1 (variations 2, 3 and 5) Medlar 2 Raisin 1 and (variations 2 and 3)	Bilberry 2 (variation 2) Bilberry 3 Blackberry 2 and (variation 2) Blackberry 3 and (variation 1)
Grape Wines	Grape 2 (variation 1) Grape 5 and (variation 1)	Grape 1 and (variation 1) Grape 2, 3 and 6	Grape 8
Flower Wines		Dandelion 1 (variation 2) Elderflower 1 Elderflower 3*	Rose Petal 2
Herb Wines		Nettle 1 (variation 1) Parsley 4 Tea 1	
Vegetable Wines	Beetroot 1	Parsnip 1	Rhubarb 1 Tomato 1

Note * Elderflower Wine 3 (page 109) is the traditional elderflower 'champagne', a moderate alcohol, summer drink.

WINE
PRESENTATION

• Labelling

Once a batch of wine is ready for drinking, clean the number of bottles that will be required in the immediate future. Replace the string or wire ties with crimped or self-shrink capsules. Choose capsule covers that indicate the type of wine.

Label the bottles with the name of the wine and the year it was made. Store the labelled bottles upright in a sectioned ex-wine carton until required.

• Serving Wine

Wines for drinking on their own, such as aperitifs and social wines are easy to choose. Table and dessert wines, on the other hand, should be chosen in relation to the food they are to accompany. If you are serving more than one wine with a meal, serve a young wine before a mature one, a dry wine before a sweet and a dry white before a red.

An astringent red wine goes well with Stilton. Conversely a light red, or even a white table wine, can complement a very mild cheese. Avoid red wines with fish like salmon, as a 'metallic' taste is induced in the mouth. A light red wine can be drunk with white fish, even though a white wine might be thought more conventional. Dessert wines also need to be chosen with care. Their flavour cannot be appreciated with sweets that are strongly flavoured with chocolate or citrus fruits.

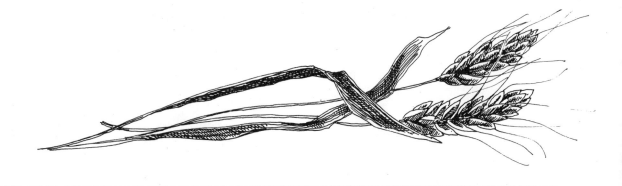

• Decanting

Twenty-four hours before serving a wine, taste a little and check it for faults such as a haze or deposit. Hazy wines cannot be cleared in time and should be replaced. Some wines form a deposit naturally with age. These are best decanted very carefully, either into a clean bottle or glass decanter.

To decant, withdraw the cork carefully, wipe the lip of the bottle with a clean cloth, hold the bottle firmly by the waist in one hand and hold the decanter or carafe in the other. Raise the bottle towards a source of light, move the lip towards the decanter or carafe until they touch, and pour the wine carefully down the inside wall. Continue pouring until the sediment slides slowly up the side of the bottle and is just about to reach the neck. Return the bottle to an upright position. Make sure the receiving vessel is left full unless the wine is slightly astringent, when a few hours in a partially filled vessel will give it a smoother flavour.

Care should be taken when removing the cork to avoid getting bits in the wine. The two-handled or the self-pulling type corkscrews are best. Wipe round the neck of the bottle with kitchen paper before pouring.

• Serving Temperature

White, rosé, sparkling wines and fino sherry are normally chilled in the refrigerator for about one hour before serving. Do not over chill good quality wines. Light red wines, such as Beaujolais and Lambrusco,

benefit from chilling (10–12°C/50–54°F). Stronger reds should be served at room temperatures (18–20°C/64–70°F). Dessert and social wines are normally served at intermediate temperatures (about 15°C/60°F).

• Glasses

A wide range of glasses is available for serving wines. All should have an incurved top to retain the bouquet. For formal occasions a selection of glasses suitable for the special qualities of the wines being served enhances the appearance of the table.

For chilled table and sparkling wines use a long-stemmed, tulip shaped glass, to keep the wines away from the warmth of the hands. Conversely, glasses for red wines have short stems and a larger bowl. Glasses for such wines are never filled more than half-full so that the wine aroma can be properly appreciated. Aperitifs and liqueurs are usually served in smaller glasses.

• Tasting Wines

Perhaps the easiest way to gauge the quality of wine produced is to compare if firstly with those of neighbours or of members of an amateur wine-making society, and then with an appropriately priced commercial wines. Many wine companies hold tastings which, for a modest fee, are very instructive.

If you are buying wines for comparison, do not start with chateau-bottled vintages but good, sound, unpretentious wines of reasonable price. When the home-made products reach this standard, then the wine-maker has also reached a reasonable standard. From then on, entry into amateur wine competitions, local, regional and national, should improve personal standards further.

When tasting a wine, it is essential to have a quiet, relaxed atmosphere, freedom from noises and any marked smells. The taster should not be suffering from a cold or catarrh.

• Flavour

To a taster the flavour of a wine is made up of several components: aroma or smell; taste; texture; the circumstances in which it is being tasted and those in which the same flavour was experienced before and general knowledge of wine flavours.

Aroma is assessed by breathing air from over the wine and across specially sensitive areas at the back of the nose. There is no sensation once the movement of air ceases. Furthermore, the ability to detect a particular aroma diminishes rapidly with time, so that after a minute or so, it cannot be detected at all. This phenomenon is called odour or aroma fatigue. A similar change also occurs in tasting. In consequence, while the same aroma cannot be detected for the moment, a different aroma is immediately apparent.

Taste There are four detectable taste components: sweetness, acidity, saltiness and bitterness. The taste components are detected on different areas of the tongue, the first three are on the front or edge. The taste buds for bitterness are set in folds of skin at the back of the tongue. Consequently, this is the last quality of the wine to be detected.

Astringency or roughness is caused when excessive tannin in the wine reacts with the protein cells from the walls of the mouth. An excess of copper or iron in the wine will also cause an unpleasant astringency.

Texture or body This is a complex sensation made up of the amounts of sugar, alcohol and soluble solids in the wine. It is easy to imagine the difference in texture or body of a dry wine and an egg nog but, between two types of dry wine the differences can only be experienced rather than described.

• Flavour Standards

The acquisition of standards for wine is difficult. Whatever the chosen method, a systematic approach to flavour assessment is important. Each stage must be learned completely before proceeding to the next.

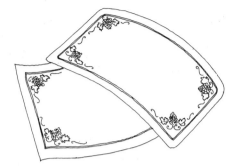

It is better to do this in a group led by an experienced wine taster or judge. Any doubts or questions can be discussed so that all the group benefits. Many wine companies now run tastings which can be of great benefit to the amateur in acquiring flavour standards.

Once trained, never be influenced by the remarks of other people tasting at the same time.

• Recording

Even wine-makers who have no intention of competing will appreciate their wines better by recording aromas and flavours. Everyone will not necessarily use the same terms, but a degree of standardisation is useful.

• Judging Wines

If it is intended to enter wines for competition it is *essential* to follow the requirements of the organising body to the letter.

The WI judging guidelines for example, are as follows: The schedule may simply request a bottle of wine, but in larger shows may specify type, e.g. red, white, rosé; table or dessert wine. Wines must be presented in clear glass punted bottles with new flanged corks which need not be sealed. Bottles should be filled to within approximately 12 mm ($\frac{1}{2}$ in.) of the base of the cork. Labels should state type of wine, year of making, and indicate sweetness. Wines should be bright in colour, characteristic and brilliantly clear. There should be no sediment in the bottle. When the cork is drawn, the wine should be stable (unless a sparkling wine). The aroma should be true, well rounded and pleasant.

Judges generally look for the following points.

Presentation First look at the unopened bottle. Is it clean and does it have the necessary cork and label requirements?

Clarity Look at the wine in the bottle against the light. Is it clear and free from any deposit?

Stability When the cork is drawn and some wine poured into the tasting glass, does it pour normally? If it was like light lubricating oil, it is spoiled microbiologically (oiliness or ropiness) and must be discarded. Deduct mark(s) for any haze in a wine pouring normally.

Was there any evidence of carbonation when the cork was removed, or in the glass of wine? Is it supposed to be a sparkling wine? If so, was there enough gas? If it is not a sparkling wine, the presence of gas is a fault. Has the wine a fresh and lively colour? Any darkening in colour in the glass indicates poor quality due to the presence of excessive amounts of iron, copper or oxidising enzymes. Discard.

Aroma The glass can then be cupped in the hands and swirled to warm the wine and so enhance its aroma. Breathe in quickly at the mouth of the glass, then take a deeper breath to confirm the first impression. Afterwards aroma fatigue sets in for that sample and sensitivity falls off rapidly. Many judges rely on one deep breath, since they regard it as more discriminating.

Some of the qualities to be looked for in the aroma can be detected very easily, e.g. slightly vinegary, oxidised, rotten eggs, diacetyl or excess sulphur dioxide. Any wine with these characteristics, even in slight amounts, is automatically graded poor in quality, if not discarded. Then there are positive qualities. The aroma can have some of the characteristics that suggest the raw material from which it was made. There should also be some components derived from fermentation. Not just crude alcohol, but the more subtle aromas of higher alcohols formed by the yeast during fermentation.

Flavour Some of the wine is rolled round the mouth for a short while, 'chewed' if necessary, air drawn over it, a little is then swallowed and the rest spat out.

The qualities of the aroma are also apparent in the taste, with some extra qualities that cannot be detected by the nose. The judge should discard any wines that are excessively oxidised (apart from Madeira or possibly sweet sherry-type wines) and similarly, any with a filter pad taste. Some flavours are only apparent after the wine has been swallowed. These include the flavours of iron, copper and 'mousiness' (page 154) all of which are extremely objectionable. Not everyone is equally sensitive to all flavours, sometimes this is genetic in origin as opposed to insufficient training.

Not only should there be any absence of faults, but the *taste balance* should be satisfactory. In general, no one quality should stand out above others. A dry, white wine should not be excessively acid, or have more than a hint of sweetness. No wine should be excessively astringent or bitter since it can be balanced by alteration of the amounts of acid and/or sugar.

The amount of *alcohol* is also important. If the content is too low it fails to give wine its true character. Excessive alcohol gives a raw, burning sensation to the palate, or can take a wine out of its declared class.

A wine should please both in its first taste and in its *after-taste*. A wine that is 'nice' to begin with, but leaves no memory, no nutty taste, no mellowness in the mouth, is only a young wine or one of little character. This is the area where only practice and experience can help. Only repeated comparisons with other wines will supply the knowledge required to analyse and mentally judge their special flavours.

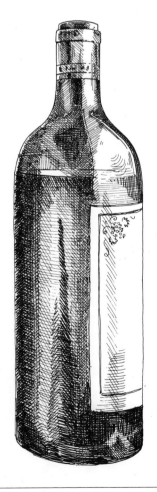

FRUIT WINES

*F*ruit wines are probably the easiest types of wine to make apart from those using concentrates. Use unblemished fruits wherever possible that are just ripe and in perfect condition. If using damaged fruit cut away and discard the bruised and damaged parts. To make good wine, good fruit must be used.

The best wine is achieved by balancing the acidity and flavour of the fruit with the other ingredients. Using different varieties of the same cultivated fruit can bring about changes in flavour. With each recipe some indication is given as to the type of wine produced and its colour. When making spiced wines, use the form of spice recommended (never use powdered) and suspend in a muslin bag in the extract or fermentation.

Frozen fruit (page 20) can be used. Allow it to thaw overnight in a plastic bin in which the recommended number of Campden tablets and acid (lemon or orange juice), dissolved in about 600 ml/1 pint of water, have been added. The fruit will break down easily the next morning when pulped, pressed, steamed or extracted with water.

Canned fruit, including the syrup, is also convenient to use. First measure the volume of the liquid and deduct 70 g/2½ oz sugar from the amount in the recipe for every 100 ml/3½ fl oz syrup. If the fruit is canned in juice, use the total weight of fruit and juice as though it were all raw material. Treat fruit pulps similarly.

A smaller quantity of dried fruit is needed than fresh, since most of the natural water content has been removed already. For every 1 kg/ 2 lb of fresh fruit specified, use 250 g/½ lb of dried. Dried fruit should be minced roughly and extracted with several small batches of water, leaving the mixture to stand for 12 hours each time before squeezing out the extract. Make up to the same volume as given in the recipe, after adding the other specified ingredients.

· APPLE WINE 1 ·

(white, sweet, country wine)

3 kg/6 lb windfall apples
water
2 Campden tablets
pectic enzyme
wine yeast
nutrients
1½ kg/3 lb white sugar

Cut out and discard any bruised and blemished segments. Wash the apples, cut up into small pieces and place in a plastic bin. Just cover with lukewarm water (25°C/75°F) in which the Campden tablets have been dissolved. Add the pectic enzyme and stir well. Cover with cling film and leave overnight.

The next day add the yeast and nutrients and stir again. Leave for five days at 20°C/70°F, stirring several times a day. Strain off the liquid, gently squeeze out the residue and discard. Add the extract to the first liquid. Stir in the sugar and make up to 5 litres/1 gallon with water. Keep covered until the frothing ceases. Stir vigorously and pour into a fermentation vessel. Insert an airlock and keep at 20°C/70°F until gas bubbles cease to form.

Continue as directed for a sweet wine on page 45.

Variations

1. *Crab apples* such as John Downie can be substituted for windfalls.
2. Brown sugar will give a fawn colour and fuller flavour to the wine.

· APPLE WINE 2 ·

(fawn, sweet, spiced, country wine)

1 kg/2 lb white sugar
4 litres/6 pints draught cider
500 g/1 lb raisins, chopped
1 Campden tablet (optional)
1 stick cinnamon, crushed
30 g/1 oz root ginger, bruised
wine yeast
nutrients
water

The addition of a yeast is suggested to ensure that a reasonable amount of alcohol is produced. If only still, draught cider is available (i.e. not cloudy and naturally conditioned), a Campden tablet must be added per 5 litres/1 gallon, followed by the yeast the next day.

Dissolve the sugar in the cider, add the raisins (and crushed Campden tablet if still cider) and suspend in it the crushed spices in a muslin bag. Leave for five days in a covered bin, adding the yeast and nutrients on the second day. On the fifth day gently squeeze the raisins and bag. Add the extract to the bulk of the liquid.

Pour into a fermentation vessel, make up to volume with water (5 litres/1 gallon), if necessary. Keep at about 20°C/70°F.

Fermentation may be slow but should proceed steadily. The liquid will probably cease fermenting while still slightly sweet. If not sweet enough, sweeten to taste. If, however, it does ferment to dryness, add 250 g/½ lb white sugar per 5 litres/ 1 gallon and in either case continue as directed for a sweet wine on page 45.

Variation

Substitute draught or bottled *perry* for cider and use the recipe above omitting the raisins and spices. Finish as directed for a dry wine on page 44.

· APPLE WINE 3 ·

(*pale fawn, sweet, spiced, country wine*)

3 kg/6 lb windfall apples
2 Campden tablets
250 g/½ lb raisins, chopped
water
1½ kg/3 lb white sugar
1 lemon, rind
15 g/½ oz root ginger
wine yeast
nutrients

Cut the apples into very thin slices, drop them into a bin with the crushed Campden tablets and raisins. Pour over 2½ litres/½ gallon boiling water, cover and leave for two days, stirring the mixture at intervals.

Squeeze out the pulp and pour the liquid into a jar; refrigerate. Return the pulp to the bin. Gently boil 2½ litres/½ gallon water for half an hour with the sugar, lemon rind and ginger. The ginger should be crushed, put in a muslin bag and held suspended in the boiling liquid. Add more water, if necessary, to restore the original volume (2½ litres/½ gallon). While still boiling, pour over the pulp and leave covered for another two days, stirring occasionally.

Squeeze out the mixture and pour this second extract with the first into a lidded fermentation bin. Discard the pulp. Warm the combined extracts to 15–20°C/60–70°F, add the yeast and nutrients. If necessary make up to volume with water (5 litres/1 gallon) and cover with the lid or cling film. When frothing ceases run into a fermentation vessel, insert the air-lock and allow to ferment completely.

Continue as directed for a sweet wine on page 45.

Treat the wine with pectic enzyme if it does not clear readily during storage.

Variations

1. Reduce the weight of sugar to 1 kg/2 lb and increase the amount of raisins to 1 kg/2 lb.
2. Substitute white grape concentrate (245 g/8½ oz) for raisins, or reduce the sugar to 1 kg/2 lb and add 490 g/17 oz concentrate per 5 litres/1 gallon.
3. Substitute *pears* for apples. Use neutral dessert pears, just starting to ripen, or perry pears. Increase the quantity of raisins to 1 kg/2 lb and the sugar to 1 kg/ 2 lb. This wine may not ferment completely.

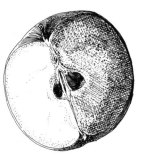

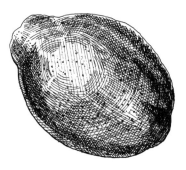

· APPLE WINE 4 ·

(white, dry, table wine)

2½ litres/4 pints white cloudy apple juice
625 g/1¼ lb white sugar
2 Campden tablets
pectic enzyme
wine yeast
nutrients
water

Empty the juice into a bin and then dissolve in the sugar and Campden tablets and add the pectic enzyme. Leave overnight. The next day add the yeast and nutrients, make up to volume with water (5 litres/1 gallon), cover and keep at 15–20°C/60–70°F.

When the frothing ceases, stir vigorously, pour into a fermentation vessel, insert the air-lock and keep at 15–20°C/60–70°F. Leave until the gas bubbles cease to form. Taste to ensure the wine is dry (completely fermented), if not treat as for a 'stuck' fermentation (page 148).

Continue as directed for a dry wine on page 44.

· APPLE WINE 5 ·

(white, dry, table wine)

3 kg/6 lb dessert apples
water
2 Campden tablets
pectic enzyme
wine yeast
1¼ kg/2½ lb white sugar
nutrients

Do not use over-ripe apples or the pulp will be difficult to press out.

Slice the apples thinly or dice, and drop into a bin containing 4 litres/6 pints water in which the Campden tablets have been dissolved. Add the pectic enzyme and leave overnight. The next morning add the yeast. Cover the bin and keep at about 15–20°C/60–70°F, squashing the pulp at intervals to free the juice. When the slices are transparent (about 3–5 days) squeeze out or press and dissolve the sugar and nutrients in the juice.

Pour the juice into a fermentation vessel, make up to volume with water (5 litres/1 gallon) and insert the air-lock.

Continue to keep warm until gas bubbles are no longer formed.

Continue as for a dry wine on page 44.

Variations

1. Use 2 kg/4 lb cooking apples as an alternative. Press the mixture of ground pulp and dissolved Campden tablets in a small fruit press, add the pectic enzyme and yeast the next day. Make up the volume with water (5 litres/1 gallon) in a fermentation vessel and ferment at 15–20°C/60–70°F and continue as above.

2. Substitute 3 kg/6 lb *pears* for the apples. They are best in flavour just before they ripen and while they are still firm. Follow the above recipe and fine with Bentonite (page 26) if the wine does not clear immediately on storage. For a more vinous and crisp flavoured wine, substitute 500 g/1 lb Bramley's seedling apples for 500 g/1 lb pears.

3. Use 2¼ kg/4½ lb dessert apples and 750 g/1½ lb *quince*. Add 3 Campden tablets and 1 kg/2 lb white sugar. Alternatively use 3 kg/6 lb quince and no apples. Blend this wine in suitable proportions with other white wines.

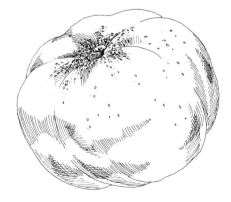

· APRICOT WINE 1 ·

(fawn, sweet, social wine)

1 kg/2 lb apricots (fresh)
water
2 Campden tablets
pectic enzyme
wine yeast
1⅓ kg/2¾ lb white sugar
nutrients

Cut out and discard any rots from the apricots and drop the halved and de-stoned fruit into a bin. Pour on 4 litres/6 pints boiling water in which the Campden tablets have already been dissolved. Cool to 30°C/85°F, mix in the pectic enzyme and mash the fruit with a wooden spoon. Cover and leave overnight. The next day keep the temperature at about 20°C/70°F and add the yeast. Cover and leave for three days (or until frothing becomes minimal), stirring at intervals.

Strain off the pulp and squeeze out gently. Combine the extract with the main bulk of liquid and dissolve in it the sugar and nutrients. Make up to volume with water (5 litres/1 gallon), pour into a fermentation vessel and insert the air-lock. Keep at 15–20°C/60–70°F until gas bubbles cease to form.

Continue as directed for a sweet wine as on page 45.

Variation

Fresh *nectarines*, *peaches*, *redcurrants* and *whitecurrants* (with the stalks removed rather than halving the fruit as above) can be substituted for apricots.

· APRICOT WINE 2 ·

(fawn, sweet, social wine)

500 g/1 lb apricots (dried)
water
2 Campden tablets
245 g/8½ oz white grape concentrate
1 kg/2 lb white sugar
nutrients
pectic enzyme
wine yeast

Chop the fruit and pour on 2 litres/3 pints boiling water in which the Campden tablets have just been dissolved. Leave overnight and then strain. Set the liquid to one side. Add another 2 litres/3 pints boiling water to the pulp and leave overnight. Strain gently and add the liquid to the first. Discard the pulp. Mix in the grape concentrate, sugar and nutrients, add the pectic enzyme and make up to volume with water (5 litres/1 gallon). Add the yeast and leave in a covered vessel and keep at about 15–20°C/60–70°F until the frothing ceases.

Mix well and pour into the fermentation vessel. Insert the air-lock and keep it at 15–20°C/60–70°F until the gas bubbles cease to form.

Continue as directed for a sweet wine on page 45.

Variations

1. Drop the cut up pieces of apricot into 3 litres/5 pints boiling water and simmer gently for half an hour. Strain through a sieve, but do not press, and discard the pulp. Dissolve the Campden tablets, pectic enzyme, sugar, concentrate and nutrients in the liquid. Leave overnight, add the yeast the next day and continue as above.
2. Dried *peaches* and *nectarines* can be substituted for apricots.

Sparkling wines are made by slightly sweetening a base wine and allowing a secondary fermentation to take place in a sealed bottle.

WHITE SPARKLING
WINE
(GRAPE)

◆ APRICOT WINE 3 ◆

(fawn, sweet, social wine)

1 kg/2 lb apricots (canned)
245 g/8½ oz white grape concentrate (optional)
water
2 Campden tablets (optional)
pectic enzyme
wine yeast
1⅓ kg/2¾ lb white sugar
nutrients

If the apricots are canned in fruit juice, add the white grape concentrate. Pour the syrup (or fruit juice plus concentrate) into the fermentation vessel. Crush the fruit roughly, or put briefly in a food processor. Pour 2 litres/3 pints hot water over the crushed fruit, allow to cool to 30°C/85°F and add the crushed Campden tablets (optional) and the pectic enzyme.

Keep covered overnight and add the yeast the next morning. Leave for three days at 20°C/70°F then strain. Run the liquid into the fermentation vessel containing the syrup/juice. Add the sugar and nutrients dissolved in sufficient water to make up to volume (5 litres/1 gallon). Insert the air-lock and keep at 15–20°C/60–70°F until gas bubbles cease to form.

Continue as directed for a sweet wine on page 45.

Variations

1. Canned *loganberries* or *raspberries* can be substituted for apricots using 1–1½ kg/2–3 lb per 5 litres/1 gallon.
2. Canned and bottled *nectarines*, *peaches* and *pineapple* can also be substituted for apricots in the above recipe.

Above: Wine tastings are very instructive for gauging the quality of home-produced wine. *Below left:* Wine glasses should have an incurved top to retain the bouquet. *Below right:* Wines containing sediment are best decanted.

· BANANA WINE ·

(light fawn, sweet, social wine)

1¼ kg/3 lb bananas
water
1⅓ kg/2¾ lb white sugar
245 g/8½ oz white grape concentrate
2 Campden tablets
nutrients
10 g/⅓ oz citric acid
starch enzyme
wine yeast

Bananas contain starch which produces a dense haze and heavy foam during fermentation. By using very ripe fruit (black skins) and the starch enzyme, the wine clears and improves noticeably on longer storage.

Skin the bananas and chop the fruit. Put the fruit and about one tenth the weight of skins in a muslin bag. Suspend the bag in a large saucepan containing 4 litres/6 pints water and bring to the boil. Simmer gently for 30 minutes, and then pour the liquid over the sugar, grape concentrate, crushed Campden tablets, nutrients and citric acid. Add any liquid gently squeezed out from the bag. If necessary, make up to volume with water (5 litres/1 gallon) and cover. When the must has cooled to 20°C/70°F add the starch enzyme and the next day the yeast. Cover and leave for at least a week, stirring at intervals and maintaining the temperature. As the must is very hazy it will be difficult to see visually when fermentation has ceased. In order to check that all the sugar has been fermented taste at intervals or use the Clini-test (page 50).

When fermentation has ceased, remove to a cool place. After one week pour into a storage jar and insert the storage bung. Leave until most of the suspended material has settled out (this can be several months). Syphon off the liquid, sweeten to taste. Fill a fermentation vessel, insert the air-lock and return to the warmth. Keep at 15–20°C/60–70°F and continue as directed for a sweet wine on page 45.

The lengthy period of storage, between the main fermentation and that designed to stabilise the sweetness, allows most of the sediment to be removed.

Variation

Use the juice of two lemons instead of the citric acid.

· BILBERRY WINE 1 ·

(red, dry, table wine)

1 kg/2 lb bilberries (fresh or bottled)
water
2 Campden tablets
10 g/⅓ oz citric acid
pectic enzyme
1¼ kg/2½ lb white sugar
wine yeast
nutrients

Crush the bilberries (also known as whortle-berries) in a fermentation bin, add 4 litres/6 pints cold water in which the Campden tablets and citric acid have been dissolved. Leave overnight and stir in the pectic enzyme, sugar, yeast and nutrients. Add water almost to volume (5 litres/1 gallon). Cover and keep at 20–25°C/70–75°F for five days, stirring several times a day. Mix, strain and pour the liquid into a fermentation vessel. Make up to volume, insert the air-lock and keep warm until gas bubbles cease to form.

Continue as directed for a sweet wine on page 45.

This recipe makes a full-bodied red wine. It can be drunk young but deserves being kept at least a year in the bottle.

Variation

Blueberries and *cranberries* can be substituted for bilberries (fresh or canned). The berries are low in acid so the amount of citric acid may need to be doubled if the wine is too insipid.

· BILBERRY WINE 2 ·

(red, dry, table wine)

350 g/¾ lb bilberries (dried)
2 Campden tablets
1¼ kg/2½ lb white sugar
nutrients
10 g/⅓ oz citric acid
water
pectic enzyme
wine yeast

Put the bilberries, Campden tablets, sugar, nutrients and acid in a bin and pour on 4 litres/6 pints boiling water. When the must cools to 30°C/85°F add the pectic enzyme and, the next morning, stir in the yeast. Cover and keep for one week at 20–25°C/70–75°F, stirring three times a day. Strain, (save the pulp for Bilberry Wine 3, variation) pour the liquid into a fermentation vessel and make up to volume with water (5 litres/1 gallon). Insert the air-lock and continue keeping warm until gas bubbles cease to form.

Continue as directed for a dry wine on page 44.

Variation

Blueberries and *cranberries* can be substituted for bilberries.

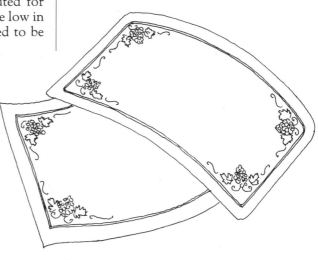

· BILBERRY WINE 3 ·

(rosé, dry, table wine)

water
500 g/1 lb bilberries fresh *or* 125 g/¼ lb dried
2 Campden tablets
pectic enzyme
nutrients
10 g/⅓ oz citric acid
wine yeast
1 kg/2 lb white sugar

Add 4 litres/6 pints cold water to crushed fresh bilberries, the crushed Campden tablets, the pectic enzyme, nutrients and citric acid.

Alternatively, put the dried bilberries into a saucepan, add the same amount of water and the acid. Heat to boiling and simmer for five minutes. Strain, add the crushed Campden tablets to the liquid to which, when it has cooled to 30°C/85°F, the pectic enzyme is added.

Leave either mixture overnight and then add the yeast and cover. Leave for three days, strain off the fruit and dissolve the sugar in the liquid. Run the liquid into a fermentation vessel and make up to volume with water (5 litres/1 gallon). Insert the air-lock and keep at at 20–25°C/70–75°F until gas bubbles cease to form.

Continue as directed for a dry wine on page 44.

Variation

Use the pulp from Bilberry Wine 2 and add 245 g/8½ oz red grape concentrate, 1¼ kg/2½ lb white sugar, 10 g/⅓ oz citric acid, 4 litres/6 pints water and the two Campden tablets.

Keep in a covered vessel and leave overnight. Add the yeast the next day and keep at 20–25°C/70–75°F until the frothing ceases. Strain, run into a fermentation vessel, make up to volume (5 litres/1 gallon) with water, insert the air-lock and keep warm until gas bubbles cease to form. Continue as directed for a dry wine on page 44.

· BLACKBERRY · WINE 1

(rosé, dry, table wine)

1½ kg/3 lb blackberries
water
3 Campden tablets
pectic enzyme
1¼ kg/2½ lb white sugar
wine yeast
nutrients

Wash and drain the berries, place in a bin and cover with boiling water in which the Campden tablets have just been dissolved.

When cool add the pectic enzyme and allow to stand covered for two days, stirring several times a day. Strain, dissolve the sugar in the juice and add the yeast and nutrients. Pour into a fermentation vessel, make up to volume with water (5 litres/1 gallon). Keep at 20–25°C/70–75°F and insert the air-lock when the frothing ceases. Allow to ferment until gas bubbles cease to form. Continue as directed for a dry wine on page 44.

Variations

1. Put the fruit in a double saucepan with a little water. Heat the water in the outer compartment to 70°C/160°F until the juice runs freely from the fruit. Strain, add the crushed Campden tablets and nutrients to the juice, stir to dissolve. Add the pectic enzyme when the juice cools and leave overnight.

The next day, dissolve the sugar in the juice, pour into a fermentation vessel, yeast and make up to volume with water (5 litres/1 gallon). Keep at 20–25°C/70–75°F and insert the air-lock when frothing ceases. Keep warm until gas bubbles cease to form, then continue as directed for a dry wine on page 44.

2. *Boysenberries, loganberries* and *mulberries* can all be substituted for blackberries. Use 3 Campden tablets for mulberry wine. *Strawberries* can also be substituted, using 1 kg/2 lb white sugar per 5 litres/1 gallon.

· BLACKBERRY ·
WINE 2

(deep red, dry, table wine)

5 kg/10 lb blackberries
pectic enzyme
3 Campden tablets
water
wine yeast
nutrients
1 kg/2 lb white sugar

Cultivated blackerries (except the Oregon Thornless) do not usually have the strong characteristic flavour of the wild hedgerow fruit and make a softer, vinous wine without the slight astringent aftertaste of the latter.

Pulp, crush or break up the fruit or briefly place in a food processor. Put the pulp in a bowl, add the pectic enzyme and the Campden tablets dissolved in a little hot water. Mix thoroughly, cover, leave overnight and add the yeast and nutrients the next morning. Keep at 20–25°C/70–75°F, stirring several times daily until the liquid has a good, rich red colour.

Squeeze and discard the pulp, dissolve the sugar in the liquid and then pour into a fermentaion vessel. Make up to volume with water (5 litres/1 gallon), insert the air-lock, and maintain the temperature until gas bubbles cease to form.

Continue as directed for a dry wine on page 44.

The dry wine should continue to be stored in a cool place for at least two years after its second syphoning or racking. Syphon off again should any further deposit form. A short storage in a scrupulously clean oak cask will give greater depth of flavour.

Taste the wine at the end of the storage period. It should be dry, full-bodied, with a rich but not obtrusive blackberry flavour. Any deficiency in acid can be corrected by adding 5 g/$\frac{1}{6}$ oz malic acid after syphoning off from the storage jar. Bottle and store another year, if possible, before drinking.

Variations

1. Frozen, canned and bottled blackberries can also be used.

2. Use 2$\frac{1}{2}$ kg/5 lb blackberries and 1$\frac{1}{4}$ kg/2$\frac{1}{2}$ lb sugar to produce a full-bodied wine with a less pronounced flavour.

3. *Mulberries* can be substituted for blackberries. To make a port allow to ferment until the specific gravity reaches 1.045, when three parts of brandy are added to five parts of fermenting juice. A less expensive version is to add one part of brandy to every three parts of wine. Fine or filter and store in a jar or a clean, old, wooden cask, with a slight air space under the seal until the flavour is smooth and luscious. Store as for a dry wine.

4. To make a sweet wine, increase the initial amount of sugar to 1$\frac{1}{2}$ kg/3 lb and finish off as for a sweet wine on page 45.

5. *Boysenberries* can be substituted for blackberries. *Raspberries* and *loganberries* can also be used, but only 1 kg/2 lb of fruit per 5 litres/1 gallon is needed.

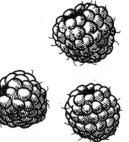

· BLACKBERRY ·
WINE 3

(rosé, dry, table or sweet, social wine)

1 kg/2 lb blackberries
5 litres/1 gallon unoxidised (white) table wine, apple, gooseberry, grape or whitecurrant
water

Steep 1 kg/2 lb crushed blackberries in the table wine until sufficient colour has been extracted. Strain and run the coloured wine into a fermentation vessel. If necessary, make up to volume with water (5 litres/1 gallon), insert an air-lock and keep at 20–25°C/70–75°F until any fermentation ceases.

Continue as directed for a dry or sweet wine as preferred, pages 44 and 45 respectively.

Variation

Bilberries, boysenberries, elderberries, loganberries, pineapple, raspberries and *redcurrants* (with the stalks removed and the berries crushed) *strawberries* and, 250 g/½ lb dried *bilberries* can all be substituted for blackberries.

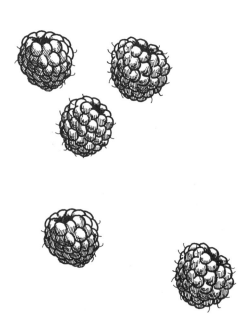

· BLACKBERRY ·
WINE 4

(red, sweet, spiced, country wine)

2 lemons, rind and juice
15 g/½ oz root ginger
6 cloves
1 stick cinnamon
water
1½ kg/3 lb white sugar
2 kg/4 lb blackberries
3 Campden tablets
pectic enzyme
wine yeast
nutrients

Put the thinly peeled lemon rind, bruised or crushed spices in a muslin bag and suspend in 4 litres/6 pints water in a saucepan. Add the sugar and bring to the boil simmering gently for 30 minutes.

Remove the bag and pour the hot liquid over the washed and drained berries. When cool, dissolve the Campden tablets in the liquid and add the lemon juice and pectic enzyme. Cover and leave overnight. The next day add the yeast and nutrients and keep at 20–25°C/70–75°F, still under cover.

Leave for two days, stirring several times a day. Strain off the pulp, pour the liquid into a fermentation vessel and make up to volume with water (5 litres/1 gallon). Insert the air-lock and keep warm until gas bubbles cease to form. Continue as directed for a sweet wine on page 45.

Variation

Substitute 1 kg/2 lb fresh *elderberries* or *redcurrants* (with the stalks removed), *loganberries* or 250 g/½ lb dried *bilberries* for the blackberries.

· BLACKCURRANT ·
WINE 1

(light red, dry, table wine)

500 g/1 lb blackcurrants
Rohament P (optional)
pectic enzyme
1½ Campden tablets
water
wine yeast
nutrients
1¼ kg/2½ lb white sugar

Blackcurrants have a very high acidity and a strong characteristic flavour. However, by using only a small amount of fruit, this recipe consistently gives a satisfactory wine that can be drunk within three months of complete fermentation.

Collect blackcurrants on a dry day when fully ripe. Wash the currants and pulp, crush or briefly use a food processor to break up the fruit. If the pulp is very viscous add the enzyme Rohament P as well as the normal pectic enzyme. Add the Campden tablets, dissolved in a little hot water, mix thoroughly and leave covered overnight. Add the yeast and nutrients the next morning. Keep at 20–25°C/70–75°F, stirring several times daily, until the liquid has a sufficiently red colour.

Strain off the pulp, dissolve the sugar in the liquid and then pour into a fermentation vessel. Make up to volume (5 litres/1 gallon) with water, insert the air-lock and keep at the same temperature until the gas bubbles cease to form. After fermentation treat as directed for a dry wine on page 44.

Variation

Use a mixture of 500 g/1 lb blackcurrants and 1 kg/2 lb redcurrants to reduce the blackcurrant flavour further.

· BLACKCURRANT ·
WINE 2

(red, sweet, social wine)

1½ kg/3 lb raisins
water
1 kg/2 lb blackcurrants, crushed
1½ Campden tablets
500 g/1 lb white sugar
nutrients
pectic enzyme
wine yeast

Wash and drain the raisins and pour on 1¼ litres/ 2 pints boiling water. When cool, strain off the liquid and reserve. Chop the swollen raisins coarsely and then scald with another 1¼ litres/ 2 pints boiling water. When cool, strain off the liquid and add to the first. Repeat a third time and discard the pulp.

Put the crushed blackcurrants with 600 ml/ 1 pint water in the centre of a double saucepan. Heat the water in the outer saucepan to boiling, then simmer until the juice runs freely. Squeeze out the juice and add to the raisin extract. Discard the fruit residue.

Dissolve the Campden tablets, sugar and nutrients in the combined liquids. When cool, pour into a fermentation vessel, add the pectic enzyme, make up to volume with water (5 litres/ 1 gallon), and leave overnight. Add the yeast the next day and keep at 20–25°C/70–75°F until the frothing ceases. Insert the air-lock and keep warm until gas bubbles no longer form.

Continue as directed for a sweet wine on page 45.

Variations

1. Substitute *bullaces*, *redcurrants* and *sloes* for blackcurrants using 2 Campden tablets instead of 1½.

2. Substitute ½ kg/1 lb raisins and 490 g/17 oz red grape concentrate for the raisins.

3. Substitute 1 kg/2 lb *damsons* for blackcurrants. A dry or a sweet wine can be produced according to the treatment given after the end of the main fermentation (page 44 and 45).

·CHERRY WINE 1·

(red, sweet, country wine)

5 kg/10 lb black cherries (fresh, frozen, canned or bottled)
water
3 Campden tablets
1 kg/2 lb white sugar
nutrients
pectic enzyme
wine yeast

Wash, drain (thaw) and chop the ripe cherries and simmer with a little water for one hour in a double saucepan. Press through a fine cloth or muslin. Mix the residue with a little hot water and re-squeeze.

Dissolve the Campden tablets, sugar and nutrients in the warm juice. Allow to cool to 30°C/85°F, add the pectic enzyme and pour the liquid into a fermentation vessel. Make up to volume with water (5 litres/1 gallon) and add the yeast the next day. Keep at 20–25°C/70–75°F, inserting the air-lock when the frothing ceases. Keep warm until gas bubbles no longer form.

Continue as directed for a sweet wine on page 45.

·CHERRY WINE 2·

(red, sweet, country wine)

2½ kg/5 lb sour or Morello cherries
water
2 Campden tablets
pectic enzyme
1½ kg/3 lb white sugar
nutrients
wine yeast

Chop up the clean, ripe fruit without smashing the stones. Steep in 4 litres/6 pints cold water to which the Campden tablets and pectic enzyme have been added. Leave covered for two days then squeeze through a cloth or nylon straining bag. Dissolve the sugar and nutrients in the liquid, pour into a fermentation jar and add the yeast. Make up to volume with water (5 litres/1 gallon) and keep at 20–25°C/70–75°F. Insert an air-lock when frothing ceases and keep warm until gas bubbles no longer form.

Continue as directed for a sweet wine on page 45.

This recipe gives a wine without the intense red colour of Cherry Wine 1 but it does have the delicate flavour of the fresh fruit.

Variations

1. For a dry wine with a rich flavour use 1½ kg/3 lb demerara sugar initially. Use white sugar to stabilise the sweetness of the wine.
2. Use 2 kg/4 lb of black and 1 kg/2 lb sour or Morello cherries.
3. If no sour cherries are available, blend sweet cherries or their juice with the juice of lemons, apples, black or redcurrants. Alternatively, blend the wine from sweet cherries with a wine made from one of these acid fruits.
4. *Greengages* can be substituted for cherries.

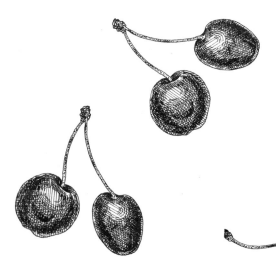

· DAMSON WINE 1 ·

(red, sweet, country wine)

2 kg/4 lb damsons (canned, bottled or fresh)
2 Campden tablets
water
pectic enzyme
wine yeast
1½ kg/3 lb white sugar
nutrients

Remove the stalks from the fresh damsons, wash and drain. Place in a bin with the crushed Campden tablets and bruise well with a wooden spoon. Add 4 litres/6 pints boiling water and leave overnight. The next day add the pectic enzyme and the yeast. Leave covered for another four days, stirring daily.

Squeeze through a muslin or nylon straining bag and dissolve the sugar and nutrients in the liquid. Pour into a fermentation vessel, make up to volume (5 litres/1 gallon) with water and keep at 20–25°C/70–75°F. When frothing ceases insert the air-lock and keep warm until gas bubbles no longer form.

Continue as directed for a sweet wine on page 45.

Variation

Greengages and *sloes* (the fruit of the blackthorn tree) can be substituted for damsons.

· DAMSON WINE 2 ·

(light red, dry, table wine)

1 kg/2 lb damsons
water
2 Campden tablets
pectic enzyme
wine yeast
nutrients
1¼ kg/2½ lb white sugar

Remove the stalks from the damsons, wash and drain. Place in a saucepan, just cover with water and bring to the boil. When cool pour into a bin, dissolve in the Campden tablets and stir in the pectic enzyme.

Add the yeast and nutrients the next day and allow to ferment for five days at 20–25°C/70–75°F, leave for longer only if a 'stone' flavour is required. Strain, dissolve the sugar in the liquid and pour into a fermentation vessel. Make up to volume with water (5 litres/1 gallon) and insert the air-lock when frothing ceases. Maintain the temperature until gas bubbles cease to form.

Continue as directed for a dry wine on page 44.

Variations

1. Use 1 kg/2 lb damsons and 500 g/1 lb elderberries (with the stalks removed) to produce a pleasing dry, slightly astringent flavour.
2. *Victoria plums, greengages* and *sloes* can be substituted for damsons.
3. A mixture of *red* and *yellow plums* will give a rosé, dry, table wine using only 1 kg/2 lb white sugar.
4. Fresh *pineapple* which has been topped and tailed and then cut into cubes can be substituted for damsons, but extend the simmering to 20 minutes. Finish off as directed for sweet wine on page 45.

· DAMSON WINE 3 ·

(full-bodied, red, dry, table wine)

2 kg/4 lb damsons
water
2 Campden tablets
pectic enzyme
1½ kg/3 lb brown sugar
nutrients
wine yeast

Remove the stalks, wash and drain the ripe fruit then cut a cross at one end. Place in a wide-necked jar or thick plastic bowl or bin. Pour on 3 litres/ 5 pints boiling water. When cool, dissolve the Campden tablets in the liquid, stir in the pectic enzyme and leave overnight. The next day dissolve the sugar and nutrients in the liquid and add the yeast. Leave for one week covered or under an air-lock. Crush the pulp at intervals without breaking the stones.

Strain into a fermentation vessel, make up to volume with water (5 litres/1 gallon), insert the air-lock and maintain at 20–25°C/70–75°F until the gas bubbles cease to form. Continue as directed for a dry wine on page 44.

· DAMSON WINE 4 ·

(red, sweet, spiced country wine)

2 kg/4 lb damsons
water
15 g/½ oz root ginger
2 Campden tablets
2 lemons, juice and rind
wine yeast
1½ kg/3 lb white sugar

Place the washed damsons in a bin and bruise. Add 4 litres/6 pints cold water, the crushed ginger root, crushed Campden tablets, lemon juice and thinly peeled rind. The next day add the yeast, cover and keep at 20–25°C/70–75°F for 10 days, stirring daily.

Strain and pour the liquid into a fermentation vessel, add the sugar and shake to dissolve. Make up to volume with water (5 litres/1 gallon), insert the air-lock and keep at 20–25°C/70–75°F until gas bubbles cease to form.

Continue as directed for a sweet wine on page 45.

· ELDERBERRY ·
WINE 1
(light red, dry, table wine)

1 kg/2 lb elderberries (fresh)
3 Campden tablets
1 lemon, juice
pectic enzyme
water
wine yeast
nutrients
1¼ kg/2½ lb white sugar

Wash the berries and remove the stalks. Crush the berries and place in a lidded bin. Add the Campden tablets dissolved in a little hot water, the lemon juice and the pectic enzyme and leave overnight with the lid on. Add 4 litres/6 pints water and the yeast. Ferment at 25°C/75°F keeping the fruit submerged.

After three days strain and collect the juice in a clean plastic bucket. Add the nutrients and sugar. Pour into a fermentation vessel, make up to volume with water (5 litres/1 gallon), insert an air-lock and keep at 25°C/75°F until gas bubbles cease to form.

Continue as directed for a dry wine on page 44.

This wine can be drunk within three months of making. It does not improve significantly in flavour after two years. There are two types of elderberry, those with red stems and small berries and those with green stems and large berries. Try both in separate wines and determine personal preference.

Variations

1. Use 500 g/1 lb damsons and 1 kg/2 lb elderberries or try blending Damson Wine 2 and Elderberry Wine 1 for a richer flavour.
2. Substitute 250 g/½ lb dried elderberries for the fresh. Soak in hot water before use.

· ELDERBERRY ·
WINE 2
(red, sweet, social wine)

1 kg/2 lb elderberries (fresh)
water
3 Campden tablets
nutrients
pectic enzyme
3 tangerines, peel and juice
wine yeast
1½ kg/3 lb white sugar

Wash the berries and remove the stalks. Place with a little water in a double saucepan. Heat the water in the outer saucepan until the juice starts to run. Transfer the contents to a bin and, when cool, add the crushed Campden tablets, nutrients, pectic enzyme and the peel and juice of the tangerines. Cover with a cloth.

The next morning add the yeast and keep at 25°C/75°F for four days. Strain, dissolve the sugar in the liquid, pour into a fermentation vessel and make up to volume with water (5 litres/1 gallon). Keep warm, inserting the air-lock when the frothing ceases. When gas bubbles cease to form continue as directed for a sweet wine on page 45.

Variations

1. Add a hot water extract of 500 g/1 lb raisins to the heated berries *or* 490 g/17 oz red grape concentrate.
2. *Cranberries* can be substituted for the elderberries. *Raspberries* can also be used, there is no need to remove the stalks.
3. As an alternative use 500 g/1 lb each of *raspberries* and *strawberries* per 5 litres/ 1 gallon or the same quantities of *raspberries* and *loganberries*.

· ELDERBERRY ·
WINE 3
(full-bodied, red, spiced, country wine)

1 kg/2 lb elderberries (fresh)
water
3 Campden tablets
1 lemon
15 g/½ oz root ginger
5 cm/2 in. cinnamon stick
8 g/¼ oz cloves
1½ kg/3 lb brown sugar
wine yeast
250 g/½ lb raisins

Wash the elderberries, remove the stalks, place the berries in a bin and pour on 4 litres/6 pints boiling water. Dissolve the Campden tablets in the liquid. Leave for two days stirring daily and then strain.

Slice the lemon, bruise the ginger and tie in a piece of muslin with the cinnamon and cloves. Boil the bag in a pint of juice for 20 minutes. When the juice is cool, lift out the bag and return the spiced juice to the main bulk.

Dissolve the sugar in the combined juices, pour into a wide-mouthed vessel, add the yeast and chopped raisins and make up to volume with water (5 litres/1 gallon), if necessary. Allow to ferment at 20°C/70°F, covering the neck of the jar with cling film, until gas bubbles cease to form. Strain and continue as directed for a sweet wine on page 45.

This is a very pleasant wine to drink on a cold winter evening. Warmed it can be served as a hot punch.

Variations

1. Substitute 2 kg/4 lb *rowanberries* per 5 litres/ 1 gallon and use the remaining ingredients or, squash the ripe berries in a bin, add the chopped raisins and pour on 2 litres/3 pints boiling water. When cold, dissolve the nutrients and Campden tablets in the liquid. Stir in the enzyme and leave covered for two days at about 20°C/70°F, stirring the mixture occasionally. Strain and reserve both pulp and liquid. Boil the sugar and crushed ginger in 2 litres/3 pints water for 20 minutes, then pour over the rowanberry/raisin pulp. Strain when cool and add the liquid to the reserved liquid. Pour into a fermentation vessel, add the yeast and make up to volume with water (5 litres/1 gallon). Keep at about 20°C/70°F until the frothing ceases, insert the air-lock and keep warm until gas bubbles cease to form. Continue as directed for a sweet wine on page 45.

2. *Sloes* can be substituted for elderberries. Follow the above recipe, but ferment on the pulp for only four days unless a 'stone' flavour is liked, in which case leave for 10 days. As an alternative to the spices use 30 g/1 oz bruised ginger root or two paprika pods or chillies.

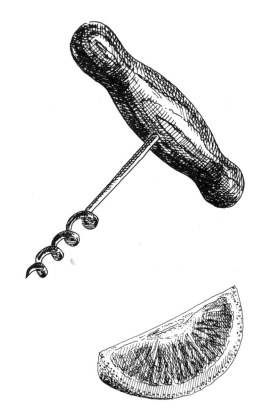

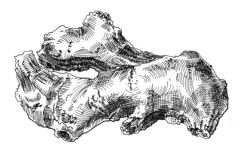

· ELDERBERRY ·
WINE 4

(full-bodied, red, sweet, social wine)

3 kg/6 lb raisins or sultanas
water
3 Campden tablets
nutrients
wine yeast
1 kg/2 lb elderberries (fresh)
pectic enzyme

Wash and chop the raisins coarsely. (Use Smyrna raisins or sultanas if possible.) Place in a bin and pour on 4 litres/6 pints cold water in which the Campden tablets and nutrients have been dissolved. Cover with cling film or insert an air-lock and leave overnight.

The next day add the yeast. Keep at 20–25°C/70–75°F for 14 days, shaking the bin each day. Remove the stalks from the elderberries and place the berries in Kilner jars. Heat in an oven to 120°C/250°F/gas mark ½ for 15 minutes or until the juice runs from the fruit. Strain the raisin wine and add 5 litres/1 gallon to each 600 ml/1 pint of strained cooled elderberry juice.

Pour the mixture, with the pectic enzyme added, into a fermentation vessel, insert the air-lock and continue to keep warm. When gas bubbles cease to form continue as directed for a sweet wine on page 45.

Variation

Substitute 1 kg/2 lb crushed *rosehips* and 150 g/6 oz *figs* for the elderberries.

· GOOSEBERRY ·
WINE

(light red, dry, table wine)

1 kg/2 lb red gooseberries
water
2 Campden tablets
pectic enzyme
wine yeast
nutrients
1¼ kg/2½ lb white sugar

Slice the gooseberries in half and drop into a bin. Pour on 4 litres/6 pints boiling water in which the Campden tablets have just been dissolved. Add the pectic enzyme when the liquid is cool and next day, the yeast and nutrients. Cover and keep at 20–25°C/70–75°F, stirring daily until the frothing ceases.

Squeeze out through muslin or a nylon straining bag and discard the pulp. Dissolve the sugar in the liquid and make up to volume with water (5 litres/1 gallon). Insert the air-lock and keep warm until gas bubbles cease to form. Continue as directed for a dry wine on page 44.

Variations

1. Add 245 g/8½ oz concentrated red grape juice per 5 litres/1 gallon with the yeast and nutrients.
2. For a white wine use large, yellow-green juicy gooseberries and add 12 chopped grape vine leaves to the pulp or 8 g/¼ oz dried elderflower florets.
3. Alternatively, add 245 g/8½ oz concentrated white grape juice per 5 litres/1 gallon with the yeast and nutrients.
4. *Strawberry* wine can also be made using this recipe. Add 1 kg/2 lb white sugar per 5 litres/1 gallon. Strain off the strawberry pulp after three days or the wine will have a woody taste.
5. *Redcurrants* and *whitecurrants* can also be substituted for gooseberries, but remove the stalks and then mince or crush the fruit.

· GRAPEFRUIT ·
WINE 1
(white/pale yellow, dry, table wine)

6 grapefruit
water
2 Campden tablets
pectic enzyme
nutrients
1¼ kg/2½ lb white sugar
wine yeast

Wash the grapefruit well. Grate the skin from one (or peel thinly or use a zester knife) into a bin and add the juice from all the fruits. Add 4 litres/6 pints water in which the Campden tablets have been dissolved. Stir in the pectic enzyme and nutrients.

The next day stir in the sugar until it dissolves and add the yeast. Keep covered at 15–20°C/60–70°F until the frothing ceases. Strain into a fermentation vessel, make up to volume with water (5 litres/1 gallon). Insert the air-lock and keep warm until gas bubbles cease to form. Continue as directed for a dry wine on page 44.

This makes a pleasant white wine whose slight astringency is conducive to good appetite. It is also a very refreshing wine for the summer and is not meant to be stored for any length of time.

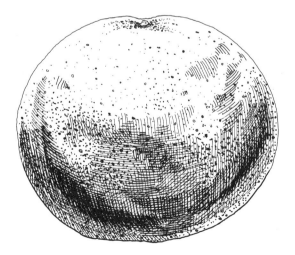

· GRAPEFRUIT ·
WINE 2
(white, dry, table wine)

700 ml/23 fl oz grapefruit juice
1¼ kg/2½ lb white sugar
nutrients
2 Campden tablets
pectic enzyme
wine yeast
water

Use unsweetened grapefruit juice free of preservatives. The volume suggested in the recipe is the equivalent to that obtained from 1 kg/2 lb of fruit.

Pour the juice into a bin, stir in the sugar, nutrients and crushed Campden tablets until dissolved. Add the pectic enzyme. Add the yeast the next day and keep at 15–20°C/60–70°F until frothing ceases. Pour into a fermentation vessel, make up to volume with water (5 litres/1 gallon), insert the air-lock and continue to keep warm until gas bubbles cease to form. Continue as directed for a dry wine on page 44. If the wine is difficult to clear, treat with Bentonite (page 26).

Variations

1. Cartons of mixed grapefruit and pineapple juice and *pineapple* juice (free from preservative) can also be used.

2. For *orange* wine use 700 ml/23 fl oz pure orange juice (or the frozen semi-concentrate after dilution to juice strength) and the remaining ingredients used above.

· HAWTHORNBERRY · WINE 1

(fawn, full-bodied, dry, table wine)

1½ kg/3 lb hawthornberries
water
3 Campden tablets
1½ kg/3 lb white sugar
nutrients
pectic enzyme
2 oranges, juice and rind
wine yeast

Wash the berries and place in a bin, pour over 4 litres/6 pints boiling water in which the Campden tablets have just been dissolved. Crush the fruit.

When cool, stir in the sugar to dissolve, together with the nutrients. Add the pectic enzyme, orange juice and thinly peeled rind. Add the yeast the next day, cover and keep at 15–20°C/60–70°F, stirring occasionally. Strain after one week, discard the pulp, pour the liquid into a fermentation vessel and make up to volume with water (5 litres/1 gallon). Insert the air-lock and keep warm until gas bubbles cease to form.

Continue as directed for a dry wine on page 44.

This wine can be bitter so it probably better drunk as a dry aperitif.

Variation

Use 245g/8½ oz white grape juice concentrate, either in addition, or in place of the oranges.

· HAWTHORNBERRY · WINE 2

(fawn, sweet, spiced, country wine)

1½ kg/3 lb hawthornberries
water
1½ kg/3 lb brown sugar
15 g/½ oz root ginger
3 Campden tablets
pectic enzyme
wine yeast
nutrients
250 g/½ lb raisins, chopped

Wash and rinse the berries. Place in a saucepan and add 4 litres/6 pints water, bring to the boil and simmer for 15 minutes. Strain and discard the pulp. Reheat the liquid with the sugar and bruised ginger root until just boiling. Allow to cool and pour into a bin, dissolve the Campden tablets in the liquid and add the pectic enzyme. The next day add the yeast, nutrients and raisins.

Keep at 15–20°C/60–70°F until the frothing ceases. Strain, pour into a fermentation jar and make up to volume with water (5 litres/1 gallon). Insert the air-lock and keep warm until gas bubles cease to form.

Continue as directed for a sweet wine on page 45.

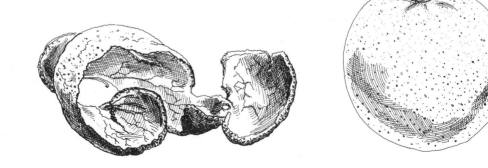

· JAM WINE ·

(the type of wine depends on the jam)

1½ kg/3 lb strawberry jam
water
2 Campden tablets
10 g/⅓ oz citric acid
pectic enzyme
500 g/1 lb white sugar
245 g/8½ oz red/rosé concentrated grape juice
nutrients
wine yeast

Jars of unwanted jam can be converted into a full-flavoured wine that tastes more mature than wine made from fresh fruit. If using commercial jams note that low sugar/sugar-free jams contain the preservatives potassium sorbate or sorbic acid which depress or prevent yeast fermentation. Ensure there are no such preservatives by carefully reading the label.

Dissolve the jam in 4 litres/6 pints warm water in a bin. When cool add the crushed Campden tablets, citric acid and pectic enzyme. Cover and leave for 24 hours (or until the pectin test is negative, page 151).

The next day stir in the sugar, concentrated juice, nutrients and yeast. Cover and allow to ferment for four days, strain and run the liquid into a fermentation vessel. Make up to volume with water (5 litres/1 gallon) and keep at 15–20°C/60–70°F, inserting an air-lock when frothing ceases. When gas bubbles cease to form, continue as directed for dry or sweet wine on pages 44 and 45.

Variation

Marmalade Wine If made from Seville oranges or grapefruit the wine will be more appropriate as an aperitif. Marmalades based on sweet oranges or tangerines, make pleasant sweet wines.

The flavour of the wine can be enhanced by adding one part of vodka (half a part of Polish white spirit) to each six parts of dry wine. Use brandy for fortifying the sweet wine.

· LEMON WINE ·

(yellow-white, sweet, country wine)

5 lemons (small), rind and juice
1½ kg/3 lb white sugar
1½ Campden tablets
nutrients
water
wine yeast

Place the lemon zest or thinly peeled rind in a bin. Dissolve the sugar, Campden tablets and nutrients in 4 litres/6 pints warm water and add to the bin. When cool, add the strained lemon juice.

Add the yeast the next day, keep covered at 15–20°C/60–70°F, stirring occasionally until frothing ceases. Strain, pour the liquid into a fermentation vessel and make up to volume (5 litres/1 gallon) with water. Insert the air-lock and continue to keep warm until gas bubbles cease to form. Continue as directed for a sweet wine on page 45.

This traditional wine is refreshing and should be drunk young.

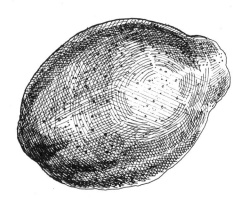

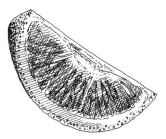

· MEDLAR WINE 1 ·

(fawn, sweet, social wine)

3 kg/6 lb medlars
500 g/1 lb raisins, chopped
1 orange, juice and rind
water
3 Campden tablets
nutrients
pectic enzyme
wine yeast
1¼ kg/2½ lb white sugar

The maximum fruit flavour is obtained by storing the medlars calyx downwards in a cool, light place until they are soft and have an acid taste with no green colour in the flesh.

Wash the fruit well, crush in a bin, add the raisins and the juice and thinly peeled orange rind. Add 4 litres/6 pints boiling water and dissolve in the Campden tablets and nutrients. Stir in the pectic enzyme using twice the amount normally recommended.

Stir in the yeast the next morning and keep at 15–20°C/60–70°F. Leave covered with a lid or cloth, stirring the mixture daily. Strain but do *not* squeeze the pulp. Let the residue roll back and forth on the stretched cloth, gradually becoming 'dewatered' in the process.

Dissolve the sugar in the liquid and pour into a fermentation vessel. Make up to volume with water (5 litres/1 gallon), insert the air-lock and keep warm until gas bubbles no longer form.

Continue as directed for a sweet wine on page 45.

· MEDLAR WINE 2 ·

(fawn, dry, table wine)

1 kg/2 lb medlars
2 kg/4 lb apples (dessert)
water
2 Campden tablets
nutrients
pectic enzyme
wine yeast
1¼ kg/2½ lb white sugar

Mash the soft ripe medlars in a bowl or bin and add the thinly sliced or grated apples, or cut both up roughly and mash with a Pulpmaster. Add 4 litres/6 pints boiling water and dissolve in the Campden tablets and nutrients. Stir in the pectic enzyme using twice the amount normally recommended.

Stir in the yeast the next morning and keep at 15–20°C/60–70°F. Leave covered with a lid or cloth, stirring the mixture daily. Strain do not squeeze the pulp. Let the residue roll back and forth, gradually becoming 'dewatered' in the process.

Dissolve the sugar in the liquid and pour into a fermentation vessel. Make up to volume with water (5 litres/1 gallon), insert the air-lock and keep warm until gas bubbles no longer form.

Continue as directed for a dry wine page 44.

· MELON WINE ·

(fawn, sweet, country wine)

2 kg/4 lb melon
3 Campden tablets
1½ kg/3 lb white sugar
nutrients
2 lemons
2 oranges
water
pectic enzyme
wine yeast

Dice the pulp and seeds of the ripe peeled melon into a bin. Add the crushed Campden tablets, sugar, nutrients and sliced lemons and oranges. Pour over 4 litres/6 pints boiling water and stir to dissolve the solids.

When cool stir in the pectic enzyme and cover. The next day add the yeast and keep covered at 15–20°C/60–70°F for five days, stirring occasionally.

Strain the liquid into a fermentation vessel, make up to volume with water (5 litres/1 gallon) and continue to keep warm. Insert the air-lock when frothing ceases and, when gas bubbles no longer form, continue as directed for a sweet wine on page 45.

· MIXED FRUIT · WINE 1

(sweet, social wine)

1 kg/2 lb dried fruit (figs, dates)
water
2 Campden tablets
3 kg/6 lb fresh fruit (apples, bananas, small citrus fruit, grapes)
pectic enzyme
nutrients
wine yeast
500 g/1 lb white sugar

Chop up the dried fruit and pour on 2 litres/3 pints boiling water in which one Campden tablet has just been dissolved. Mix thoroughly and leave overnight. The next day run off and reserve the liquid. Pour another 2 litres/3 pints boiling water, again with a Campden tablet, on the pulp. The next day squeeze the pulp to remove any surplus liquid. Discard the pulp.

Pour the combined extracts into a bin containing any spare fruit, e.g. sliced apples, bananas and any small citrus fruit. Use the zest and juice of large oranges or grapefruit and add any grapes after removing the stalks and squashing.

Stir in the pectic enzyme, nutrients and yeast; cover. Keep at about 20°C/70°F. Leave for five days or until frothing ceases. Strain the mixture and gently press out any surplus. Discard the pulp. Dissolve the sugar in the liquid, pour into a fermentation vessel and make up to volume with water (5 litres/1 gallon). Insert the air-lock and keep warm until gas bubbles cease to form.

Continue as directed for a sweet wine on page 45.

· MIXED FRUIT ·
WINE 2

(red, full-bodied, sweet dessert wine)

500 g/1 lb blackcurrants
500 g/1 lb whitecurrants
500 g/1 lb redcurrants
500 g/1 lb raspberries
500 g/1 lb cherries
2 Campden tablets
nutrients
water
pectic enzyme
wine yeast
1 kg/2 lb white sugar

Remove the stalks from the currants, place in a bin and mix with the raspberries and de-stoned cherries. Crush the fruit and dissolve the Campden tablets and nutrients in a little hot water and add to the bin with the pectic enzyme and cover. Leave the mixture overnight, add the yeast the next day and keep covered at 20–25°C/70–75°F.

After a week squeeze the mixture through a muslin or a nylon straining bag. Discard the pulp and dissolve the sugar in the liquid. Pour into a fermentation vessel and make up to volume with water (5 litres/1 gallon). Insert the air-lock. Keep warm until gas bubbles cease to form.

Continue as directed for a sweet wine on page 45.

Variation

Blackberries can be substituted for raspberries; *damsons* for cherries; *red gooseberries* for redcurrants; *grapes, elderberries and loganberries* for raspberries; *strawberries and gooseberries* for cherries.

· ORANGE WINE ·

(fawn, sweet, dessert wine)

12 sweet oranges, rind and juice
water
pectic enzyme
1½ kg/3 lb white sugar
2 Campden tablets
nutrients
wine yeast

Wash the oranges thoroughly, wipe dry, then peel thinly or remove the zest. Drop the skins or zest into a bin. Pour on 1¼ litre/2 pints boiling water and, when cool, add the orange juice, pectic enzyme and 2½ litres/4 pints cold water in which the sugar, Campden tablets and nutrients have been dissolved.

Add the yeast the next day and cover. Keep at 15–20°C/60–70°F for 3 days. Strain and discard the residue. Pour the liquid into a fermentation vessel and make up to volume with water (5 litres/1 gallon). Insert the air-lock and keep warm until gas bubbles no longer form.

Continue as directed for a sweet wine on page 45.

Variations

1. Substitute 20 clementines, satsumas or tangerines for sweet oranges. Do not peel, just slice thinly.
2. For a dry, slightly bitter aperitif substitute Seville oranges for sweet oranges *or* mix six Sevilles and six sweet oranges.
3. Add 500 g/1 lb large raisins or sultanas per 5 litres/1 gallon to 12 sweet oranges. The dried fruit is chopped and mixed with the zest or peel on which boiling water is poured.

· PEAR WINE ·

(pale fawn, sweet, social wine)

3 kg/6 lb dessert pears
3 Campden tablets
water
1⅓ kg/2¾ lb demerara sugar *or* 1½ kg/3 lb clover honey
wine yeast

Slice and squash the fruit in a bin and add the Campden tablets dissolved in 1¼ litres/2 pints water. Leave overnight and squeeze out through muslin or a nylon straining bag or a small fruit press. Discard the pulp.

Dissolve the sugar or honey in the liquid. Pour into a fermentation vessel, make up to volume with water (5 litres/1 gallon) and keep at 15–20°C/60–70°F. Insert the air-lock when frothing ceases and, when gas bubbles no longer form, continue as directed for a sweet wine on page 45.

Variation

Substitute 1 kg/2 lb white sugar and 500 g/1 lb chopped raisins for the sugar or honey. Extract the raisins with 1 litre/2 pints boiling water, strain when cool, dissolve the Campden tablets in the extract and add to the squashed pears. Continue as above.

· PLUM WINE ·

(red or fawn, sweet, spiced, country wine)

1 orange, rind and juice
1 lemon, rind and juice
6 cloves
30 g/1 oz root ginger
water
2 kg/4 lb white sugar
2 kg/4 lb plums
3 Campden tablets
pectic enzyme
wine yeast
nutrients

Put the thinly peeled orange and lemon rind, bruised or crushed spices in a muslin bag and suspend in 4 litres/6 pints water in a saucepan. Add the sugar and bring to the boil, simmering gently for 30 minutes.

Remove the bag and pour the hot liquid over the washed and drained plums in a bin. When cool, dissolve the Campden tablets in the liquid and add the orange and lemon juice, and pectic enzyme. Cover and leave overnight. The next day add the yeast and nutrients and keep at 20–25°C/70–75°F, still under cover. Leave for two days, stirring several times a day. Strain off the pulp, pour the liquid into a fermentation vessel and make up to volume with water (5 litres/1 gallon). Insert an air-lock and keep warm until gas bubbles cease to form.

Continue as directed for a sweet wine on page 45.

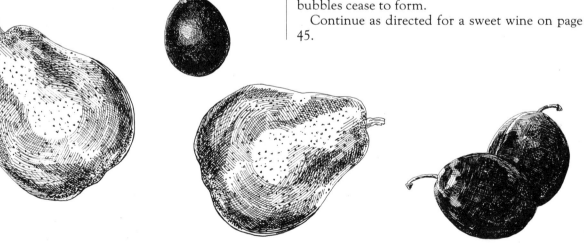

· QUINCE WINE 1 ·

(white, sweet, country wine)

2½ kg/5 lb quince
water
2 Campden tablets
2 lemons, juice and rind
1½ kg/3 lb white sugar
pectic enzyme
wine yeast

Quince are yellow, 8–10 cm/3–4 in. long. They should be left on the tree until fully ripe and gathered dry. If not used immediately, store away from other fruits as they have a strong aroma. Japanese Quince do not make such good wine.

Grate or pulp the quince and simmer in 4 litres/ 6 pints water for not more than 15 minutes. Strain into a bin containing the Campden tablets, the juice and thinly peeled lemon rind and the sugar. (Omit the lemons if the quince are very acid.) Stir to dissolve and leave covered overnight. Add the pectic enzyme and the next day the yeast; leave for another 24 hours or until frothing begins.

Strain into a fermentation vessel, make up to volume with water (5 litres/1 gallon), and keep at 15–20°C/60–70°F. Insert the air-lock when frothing ceases and keep warm until gas bubbles no longer form.

Continue as directed for a sweet wine on page 45. Blend to taste with other sweet wines if necessary.

· QUINCE WINE 2 ·

(pale fawn, sweet, social wine)

2 kg/4 lb quince
1 kg/2 lb raisins, chopped
2 Campden tablets
water
750 g/1½ lb white sugar
wine yeast

Grate, slice or pulp the ripe quince and add to a bin containing the raisins and the Campden tablets dissolved in 2 litres/3 pints boiling water. Leave covered for 24 hours, stirring at intervals. Strain off the liquid into a bin and dissolve in the sugar.

Make up to volume with water (5 litres/1 gallon) and add the yeast. Cover and keep at 15–20°C/60–70°F until the frothing ceases. Stir and pour into a fermentation vessel, insert the air-lock and keep warm until gas bubbles cease to form.

Continue as directed for a sweet wine on page 45.

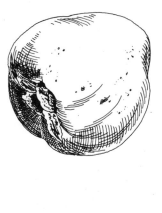

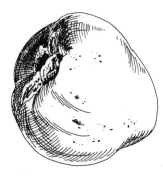

· RAISIN WINE 1 ·

(light fawn, dry, table wine)

water
500g/1 lb raisins
2 Campden tablets
pectic enzyme
1 kg/2 lb white sugar
nutrients
wine yeast

Pour 2 litres/3 pints boiling water over the raisins and dissolve one Campden tablet in the liquid. When cool, strain off the liquid and reserve. Chop the plumped-up fruit and pour on another 2 litres/3 pints boiling water, again with a Campden tablet dissolved in it. Strain when cool, discard the pulp and combine the two batches of liquid.

Add the pectic enzyme to the liquid, dissolve in the sugar and nutrients. Pour into a fermentation vessel, make up to volume with water (5 litres/1 gallon). Add the yeast the next day and keep at 15–20°C/60–70°F.

Insert the air-lock when frothing ceases and continue as directed for a dry wine page 44 when gas bubbles cease to form.

Should the wine not clarify during storage either chill and filter cold or fine with Bentonite (page 26).

Variations

1. Any insipidness can be corrected by adding 15 g/½ oz citric or malic acid to 5 litres/1 gallon wine before storage.
2. *Sultanas* can be substituted for raisins. They have a less intense flavour so it is necessary to use up to 2 kg/4 lb per 5 litres/1 gallon reducing the sugar to 500g/1 lb. Dried *currants* and *muscatels* can also be substituted for raisins.

· RAISIN WINE 2 ·

(fawn, sweet, social wine)

water
750 g/1½ lb raisins
2 Campden tablets
pectic enzyme
1 kg/2 lb white sugar
500g/1 lb white honey
nutrients
wine yeast

Pour 2 litres/3 pints boiling water over the raisins and dissolve one Campden tablet in the liquid. When cool, strain off the liquid and reserve. Chop the plumped up fruit and pour on another 2 litres/3 pints boiling water, again with a Campden tablet dissolved in it. Strain when cool, discard the pulp and combine the two batches of liquid.

Add the pectic enzyme to the liquid, dissolve in the sugar, honey and nutrients. Pour into a fermentation vessel, make up to volume with water (5 litres/1 gallon). Add the yeast the next day and keep at 15–20°C/60–70°F. Insert the air-lock when the frothing ceases. When gas bubble no longer form, continue as directed for a sweet wine on page 45.

This wine gives a flavour reminiscent of a sweet Madeira. Add one part of brandy to four parts of the wine and store in filled jars at 50°C/120°F until the wine tastes similar to Madeira.

Variation

Substitute *sultanas* for raisins using up to 2 kg/4 lb per 5 litres/1 gallon reducing the sugar to 500 g/1 lb.

· RAISIN WINE 3 ·

(dark fawn, sweet, dessert wine)

water
1 kg/2 lb raisins
2 Campden tablets
pectic enzyme
1¼ kg/2½ lb white sugar
500g/1 lb white honey
nutrients
wine yeast

Pour 2 litres/3 pints boiling water over the raisins and dissolve one Campden tablet in the liquid. When cool, strain off the liquid and reserve. Chop the plumped up fruit and pour on another 2 litres/3 pints boiling water, again with a Campden tablet dissolved in it. Strain when cool, discard the pulp and combine the two batches of liquid.

Add the pectic enzyme to the liquid, dissolve in the sugar, honey and nutrients. Pour into a fermentation vessel, make up to volume with water (5 litres/1 gallon). Add the yeast the next day and keep at 15–20°C/60–70°F.

Insert the air-lock when the frothing ceases and, when gas bubbles no longer form, continue as directed for a dry wine on page 44.

Ferment to dryness as directed and then sweeten. Wash 250 g/½ lb raisins and scald in hot water. Discard the water. Chop up the raisins coarsely, drop into 600 ml/1 pint boiling water and simmer for 20 minutes. Strain, return the liquid to the saucepan and gently re-heat until only a fairly thick syrup remains.

Add the extract to the dry wine after its first syphoning and test for pectin (page 151). If the test is positive treat with pectic enzyme. Leave for two days at 20°C/70°F or until the pectin test is negative. A more grapey flavoured wine can be made by using 245 g/8½ oz good quality white grape concentrate instead of the raisin extract.

Continue as directed for a sweet wine on page 45.

This wine gives a flavour reminiscent of a sweet Madeira. Add one part of brandy to four parts of the wine and store in filled jars at 50°C/120°F until the wine tastes similar to Madeira.

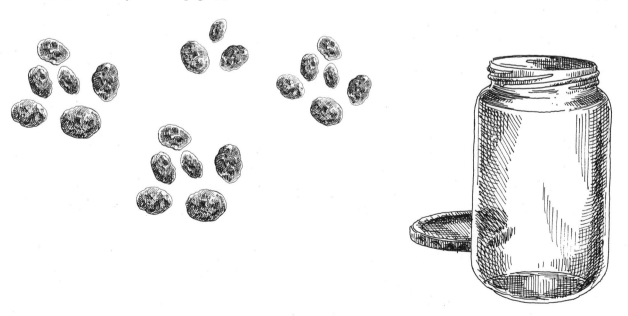

· ROSEHIP WINE 1 ·

(full-bodied, fawn, dry, table wine)

2 kg/4 lb rosehips
water
3 Campden tablets
1¼ kg/2½ lb white sugar
nutrients
pectic enzyme
2 oranges, juice and rind
wine yeast

All rosehips can be used but, to avoid reducing the number of blooms on garden hybrid roses, use instead the wild rose. Gather the rosehips after the first frost, wash and drain and place in a heavy duty plastic bag and crush. If the hips have been left to become squashy before picking, add 10 g/⅓ oz citric or malic acid to the extract to produce a fresh flavoured wine.

Place the crushed hips in a bin, pour over 4 litres/6 pints boiling water in which the Campden tablets have just been dissolved. Crush the fruit again if necessary.

When cool, stir in the sugar to dissolve, together with the nutrients. Add the pectic enzyme, orange juice and thinly peeled rind. Add the yeast the next day, cover and keep at 15–20°C/60–70°F, stirring occasionally. Strain after one week, discard the pulp, pour the liquid into a fermentation vessel and make up to volume with water (5 litres/1 gallon). Insert the air-lock and keep warm until gas bubbles cease to form.

Continue as directed for a dry wine on page 44.

Variations

1. Replace ½ kg/1 lb sugar with 490 g/17 oz white grape concentrate per 5 litres/1 gallon, or the same amount of malt extract. Chopped raisins, dried bananas or peaches are interesting variations to try. Sweet wines can be made with any one of these additions, without reducing the original quantity of sugar and following the instructions for a sweet wine (page 45).
2. Crush, dried rosehips or rosehip shells (500 g/5 litres or 1 lb/1 gallon) can be used instead of fresh.

· ROSEHIP WINE 2 ·

(full-bodied, fawn, dry, table wine)

600 ml/1 pint rosehip syrup
300 ml/½ pint pure orange juice
pectic enzyme
water
2 Campden tablets
1 kg/2 lb white sugar
nutrients
wine yeast

Pour the syrup and juice (ensure they are free of preservatives) into a fermentation vessel. Add the pectic enzyme and a little water in which the Campden tablets, sugar and nutrients have been previously dissolved. Make up to volume with water (5 litres/1 gallon).

Add the yeast the next day, keep at 15–20°C/60–70°F, inserting the air-lock when the frothing ceases and continue as directed for a dry wine (page 44) when gas bubbles no longer form.

Variations

1. The addition of 245 g/8½ oz white grape concentrate is optional.
2. Substitute *blueberries* for rosehips.

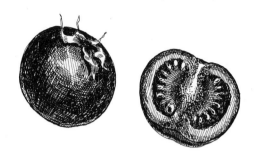

· TOMATO WINE ·

(rosé fawn, dry, table wine)

2½ kg/5 lb ripe tomatoes
water
2 Campden tablets
pectic enzyme
1 kg/2 lb white sugar
nutrients
2 lemons, juice
wine yeast

Boil the tomatoes in 2 litres/3 pints water until soft. Mash and add an equal quantity of cold water, the crushed Campden tablets, pectic enzyme, sugar, nutrients and lemon juice. Stir to dissolve the soluble ingredients.

The next day, strain, run the liquid into a fermentation vessel, add the yeast and make up to volume with water (5 litres/1 gallon). Keep at about 20°C/70°, inserting the air-lock when frothing ceases.

Continue as directed for a dry wine on page 44 when gas bubbles cease to form.

Variations

1. A sweet, social wine can be made from the same weight of tomatoes and 1½ kg/3 lb sugar, finishing off as directed for a sweet wine on page 45.
2. *Sharon fruit* or *tamarillo* can be substituted for tomatoes but use 500 g/1 lb of fruit to begin with to test personal preference and intensity of flavour.

· WHORTLEBERRY · WINE 1

(reddish fawn, sweet, spiced, country wine)

2 kg/4 lb whortleberries
30 g/1 oz root ginger, bruised
2 Campden tablets
60 g/2 oz cream of tartar
water
2½ litres/4 pints draught cider
pectic enzyme
8 g/¼ oz dried lavender
8 g/¼ oz dried rosemary
1¾ kg/3½ lb white sugar
nutrients
wine yeast

Crush the berries in a bin and add the ginger, crushed Campden tablets, cream of tartar and 2½ litres/4 pints boiling water. When cool, stir in the draught cider, pectic enzyme, the dried herbs, the sugar and the nutrients. Make up to volume with water if necessary (5 litres/1 gallon). The next day add the yeast, cover and keep at about 20°C/70°F until gas bubbles cease to form. Strain and continue for a sweet wine as directed on page 45.

Variation

Substitute *cranberries* for whortleberries. Heat the berries until they just start to pop.

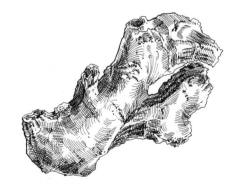

EXOTIC WINES

*T*he flavour of some of these fruits is so characteristic and strong that it is difficult to suggest recipes whose wines would have a wide appeal at an economic price. It is much easier to experiment with small quantities using the steeping method. Instead of making 5 litres/ 1 gallon with each fruit, mix 70–150 g/2½–6 oz of crushed/skinned/ destoned/deseeded fruit with one bottle (750 ml/26 fl oz) of a neutral flavoured wine. Allow to steep, tasting at intervals. Wine-makers can then decide which fruit and the amount of flavour they prefer. The flavours are a matter of individual taste. It is not difficult then to make up a large quantity of steeped wine or to choose a suitable recipe for a wine based on the fresh fruit.

The following notes on the characteristics of the fruits may be helpful in choosing which to experiment with:

Cape gooseberry Bright yellow berries with a waxy coating, surrounded by a husk which is discarded. The berry has a sweet taste, reminiscent of a blackberry.

Carambola, star apple, star fruit Shaped as its common name suggests. Pale, shiny, yellow green. Cut off pointed top and bottom and the ribbed edges. The remaining skin and pulp is edible and has a sweet-sour flavour.

Guava There are some 50 varieties, all round or pear shaped, yellow-green with a tough skin. Immature fruit has highly astringent and inedible pulp which becomes yellow and soft when fully ripe. The best sorts have a slightly sweet flavour blended with muskiness and mild acidity. The fruit can either be cut in half crossways and the pinky-white flesh and seeds scooped out, or as the skin is edible, mill or crush to a pulp, heat to 38–45°C/100–110°F and treat with a pectic enzyme overnight. Press out in a nylon straining bag or small fruit press. To make a nectar pulverise in a liquidiser or fruit processor, strain out the pips and gritty cells (like those in pears) with a fine sieve and blend two parts of pulp with seven of water and one of sugar. Acidify with a little lemon juice or citric acid if preferred. The flavour of the pulp is more acceptable blended with another juice such as apple, orange or white grape.

Kiwi fruit, Chinese gooseberry Ripe fruit are dark-reddish brown in colour, covered with red bristles and the size of a walnut or small egg. This thin woody shell is easily peeled from the berries. The flesh is bright green with many edible black seeds. Flavour something like a gooseberry.

Kumquat Tiny elongated oranges with an edible sweet skin and acid pulp. Flavour tart and aromatic rather like a tangerine.

Lychee Knobbly reddish brown, brittle skin, easily peeled off. Inside the white translucent flesh surrounds a large shiny seed. Flavour of the flesh is sub-acid and slightly akin to muscat grape with its own characteristic aroma.

Mango Round, oval, elongated or pear shaped, up to 15 cm/6 in. long. The skin is green turning yellow, rich pink or red on ripening. It has one large flattened seed surrounded by yellow to orange coloured flesh which is juicy with a rich spicy flavour. For nectar, ripe fruit is washed, peeled, cut through horizontally, the flesh eased away from the stone, put through a food processor and then a sieve. The nectar is usually flavoured with apricot and pineapple. A clear juice is not easy to prepare.

Mangosteen Small fruit with leathery skin which divides into five or seven segments. Hold in the palm and twist off half of the shell. The flesh has a characteristic taste of strawberry, peach or grape.

Papaya, pawpaw The fruit is the size of a small melon, pear shaped, and has a soft skin turning from green to yellow when ripe. The flesh is deep yellow to salmon in colour, surrounding a central cavity containing many brown-black, pea-sized seeds. It tastes very sweet, slightly scented and musky, mild and pleasant. Cut in half, scoop out the seeds and add lime juice as it is sub-acid. A nectar can be made by passing peeled, sliced, acidified fruit through a sieve, similar to tomato juice extraction. Or, remove the seeds from peeled and sliced fruit and with lime juice homogenise in a food processor.

Passion fruit, purple granadilla Purple, hard leathery skin, round or oval, the size of a small egg. The pulp is juicy, orange in colour, acidic and very aromatic, surrounding many small seeds. The pulp is extracted from the halved fruit by spooning and the seeds removed by brushing the pulp through a fine sieve. It contains starch which increases the viscosity of the juice. This is good for a nectar, but for wine the pulp would need to be heated to 55°C/130°F, cooled and treated with a starch destroying enzyme. Drinks usually contain only 5 per cent of juice, sweetened and acidified or blended with orange (most popular) or apple, because of the exceptional intensity of flavour and acidity of the single strength (yellow) juice.

Pomegranate Source of grenadine syrup. The ripe fruit is the size of an orange, has a hard yellowish brown rind and improves with long keeping. It has a sweet-acid, pink pulp surrounding many seeds. When scooped from the fruit, seed and pulp are like crystals. The juice is squeezed from the pulp of the halved or quartered fruit through muslin, but do *not* use too much pressure as the excessive tannin in the skin gives the juice a bitter taste. It is converted into a syrup with the addition of $\frac{1}{2}$ g/2 g of vitamin C (ascorbic acid) per 1 litre/1 gallon with the necessary sugar. The syrup is hot filled into bottles (see page 141) and can be drunk diluted or used for flavouring wines, other drinks and liqueurs.

Pomelo, pummelo, shaddock Largest of the citrus fruits (due mainly to the thick rind), similar to a grapefruit but more pear shaped. Flesh firm, coarse and can be pale yellow, cream or pink. Storing the fruit for some time makes the pulp more juicy and richer in flavour.

Sapodilla Small, round or egg shaped, with a brown skin. Delicious flesh, sweet and melting. Tastes like a pear or banana. Be careful of the seeds which have small hooks.

Sharon fruit Improved persimmon which, instead of being acid and full of pips, is bright orange, tomato-like, seedless and sweet. The full flavour is only developed when the pulp becomes soft, it is then orange or salmon coloured with flattened seeds (see Tomato Wine page 89).

Tamarillo, tree tomato Egg-shaped, turning from greenish-purple to orange-red when ripe. Pulp is light orange (contains black seeds) and sweeter in taste than an ordinary tomato, sub-acid and refreshing (see Tomato Wine page 89).

Ugli fruit (mixed citrus hybrid) Pinkish yellow flesh, sweeter than a grapefruit and sharper than a tangerine.

GRAPE WINES

In the UK, grape vines were first planted late in the third century A.D., but it wasn't until the seventh century when the monasteries planted vineyards, that vines were cultivated extensively. Vine cultivation went into a decline from the fourteenth century onwards until at the beginning of the nineteenth century vineyards had almost disappeared. Vineyards were planted again after the Second World War and are increasing in number. They lie in selected micro-climates, roughly south of a line from the Wash to the Severn. Some two years out of five give reduced crops because of poor summers and a number of vineyards now use polythene sheeting and tunnels to improve fruit set and ripening.

Many grape varieties, including German and French hybrids are being tried to find those most suited to our climate, as well as the optimum method of management. Most of the grapes at present are white. English white wines are modelled on the German type – white, moderate alcohol, crisp, dry or sweetened to some extent at bottling by the addition of Süssmost (stored, sulphited juice). Red wines produced so far can be of good colour and drunk reasonably young, but the best would benefit from barrel ageing which is now beginning in the best UK wineries.

• Sources of grapes

Grapes are available to the home wine-maker from several sources, fresh from the UK or imported, or as commercial products such as juices, concentrates or dried fruits. White and red grape juices are

readily available. Similarly there are concentrated juices, not only of plain white or red for making wine on their own, but also for boosting the flavour of wines made from other fruits. The quality of the wine will depend on the quality of the concentrate. At one extreme the wine from red concentrates will have a good red colour, at the other more reddish brown. From white concentrates the colour of the wine can vary from white to fawn. Concentrates are also blended by manufacturers to give wines similar to particular types, e.g. Moselle, Piesporter, Niersteiner, Sherry, Port, Madeira and Vermouth. Winemaking kits are not only suitable for making particular types of wine but some are designed to produce drinkable wine in a short time (three weeks).

• Grape Varieties

There are many varieties of grapes, derived either from natural hybridisation or from deliberate breeding programmes. Clones of varieties of various grapes have been developed to suit particular micro-climates or wine growing areas. Clones that produce a higher yield are now replacing many local varieties. Some grapes such as the Cabernet Sauvignon and Chardonnay are grown in many regions of the world.

Grapes can be classified in several ways, perhaps most obviously as white skin and flesh, coloured skin and white flesh and coloured skin and flesh. White wines can be made from the first two sorts by direct pressing. The colour of wines made from such grapes is related to the degree of oxidation received by the pulp. The amount of colour from red or black skin/white fleshed grapes is governed by the variety and the breakdown of skin cells during processing. All coloured (red skin and flesh) or teinturier grapes yield colour readily and in great quantity. They are used mainly for blending to maintain colour standards from year to year.

· GRAPE WINE 1 ·

(white, dry, table wine)

7 kg/14 lb white grapes
500 g/1 lb white sugar
pectic enzyme
2 Campden tablets
wine yeast
15 g/½ oz calcium carbonate (precipitated)

Rinse the bunches of grapes, drain and strip the berries from the stalks. Crush the berries and squeeze the pulp lightly in muslin, a nylon straining bag or a small fruit press. Measure the volume of juice and add sufficient sugar to increase the specific gravity to 1.090 (1.080 if only a light or a sparkling wine is wanted) by using the table on page 23. Otherwise add 500 g/1 lb white sugar per 5 litres/1 gallon. Add the pectic enzyme, dissolve in the Campden tablets and leave covered overnight.

Syphon off the liquid the next morning, add the yeast and pour the juice into a fermentation jar. Keep at 15–20°C/60–70°F. When the frothing ceases, clean the outside of the jar and insert the air-lock. Continue to keep warm until gas bubbles cease to form.

Remove the vessel to a cold place and leave for 14 days for the wine to clear at least partially, then syphon off the wine leaving the yeast deposit behind.

Wine from English grapes will almost certainly contain too much acid. Taste to check and, if it is too acid, stir the calcium carbonate into a little of the wine and mix it with the main bulk.

Dissolve one Campden tablet in each 5 litres/1 gallon wine and insert a storage bung. Keep the vessel as cold as possible. Crystals of tartrate will form. Syphon off the wine and store cool in a filled and sealed jar until the spring (this is traditional). Taste again. If still too acid add 5 g/½ oz BP quality potassium carbonate per 5 litres/3 gallons and again chill and syphon. Any haze in the wine can be removed by fining with Bentonite (page 26).

Dissolve one Campden tablet per 5 litres/1 gallon of clear wine, bottle, cork, capsule and store in a cold cellar. To imitate a German style wine, add clear white grape juice to taste the day before drinking. Otherwise use white sugar. Serve chilled.

Variations
1. Substitute a mixture of white and red (white fleshed) grapes for the white. Either use equal weights of each or two parts white and three red. This gives more 'body' to the wine.
2. An alternative to the reduction of acidity with calcium carbonate is the addition of 5 g/½ oz BP quality potassium carbonate to 5 litres/3 gallons of juice and again to the wine after its first syphoning if still too acid.

· GRAPE WINE 2 ·

(white, dry, traditional country wine)

2 kg/4 lb white grapes
3 Campden tablets
3 litres/5 pints water
pectic enzyme
1¼ kg/2½ lb white sugar
wine yeast
nutrients

Wash and drain the grapes, strip from the stalks and crush in a bowl or bin. Dissolve the Campden tablets in the water and pour over the pulp. Stir in the pectic enzyme. Leave covered with a cloth for three days, stirring frequently.

Strain and discard the pulp. Dissolve the sugar in the liquid, add the yeast and pour into a fermentation vessel. Make up to volume with water if necessary (5 litres/1 gallon) and keep at 15–20°C/60–70°F. When the frothing ceases, clean the outside of the vessel and insert the air-lock. Add the nutrients if fermentation is slow. Keep warm until gas bubbles cease to form.

Continue as directed for a dry wine page 44.

Above: Canned fruits are convenient to use if the fresh fruits are not available. *Below:* To experiment with the flavour of more exotic fruits, try steeping small quantities in a neutral flavoured white wine.

· GRAPE WINE 3 ·

(white, dry, table wine)

white grape juice
500 g/1 lb white sugar
pectic enzyme
2 Campden tablets
wine yeast
15 g/½ oz calcium carbonate (precipitated)

Use commercial white grape juice free from preservatives. Measure the volume of juice and add
sufficient sugar to increase the specific gravity to
1.090 (1.080 if only a light or a sparkling wine is
wanted) by using the table on page 23. Otherwise
add 500 g/1 lb white sugar per 5 litres/1 gallon.
Add the pectic enzyme, dissolve in the Campden
tablets and leave overnight.

Syphon off the liquid the next morning, add the
yeast and pour the juice into a fermentation jar.
Keep at 15–20°C/60–70°F. When the frothing
ceases, clean the outside of the jar and insert the
air-lock. Continue to keep warm until the gas
bubbles cease to form.

Remove the vessel to a cold place and leave for
14 days for the wine to clear at least partially.
Syphon off the wine leaving the yeast deposit
behind. Taste to check if the wine is too acid. If it
is too acid stir the calcium carbonate into a little
of the wine and mix it with the main bulk. Dissolve one Campden tablet in each 5 litres/1 gallon
of wine and insert a storage bung. Keep the vessel
as cold as possible. Crystals of tartrate will form.
Syphon off the wine and store cool in a filled and
sealed jar until the spring. Taste again. If still too
acid add 5 g/½ oz BP quality potassium carbonate
per 5 litres/3 gallons and again chill and syphon.

If the wine does not need acid reduction, cool
for six months in a filled and sealed jar. Any haze
in the wine can be removed by fining with
Bentonite (page 26). Bottle, cork, capsule an store
the wine in a cold cellar.

Variation

Use clear *red grape juice* and the ingredients and
method above.

· GRAPE WINE 4 ·

(white, sweet, social wine)

7 kg/14 lb white grapes
500 g/1 lb white sugar
pectic enzyme
2 Campden tablets
wine yeast
15 g/½ oz calcium carbonate (precipitated)

Rinse the grapes, drain and strip the berries from
the stalks. Crush the berries and squeeze the pulp
lightly. Measure the volume of juice and add sufficient sugar to increase the specific to 1.090 by
using the table on page 23. Otherwise add 500 g/
1 lb white sugar per 5 litres/1 gallon. Add the
pectic enzyme, dissolve in the Campden tablets
and leave covered overnight.

Syphon off the liquid the next morning, add the
yeast and pour the juice into a fermentation jar.
Keep at 15–20°C/60–70°F. When the frothing
ceases, clean the outside of the jar and insert the
air-lock. Continue to keep warm until gas bubbles
cease to form. Dissolve 250 g/½ lb white sugar in
each 5 litres/1 gallon. Reinsert the air-lock and
keep at 15–20°C/60–70°F.

Continue as directed for a sweet wine on page
45. When stabilised taste the wine. If it is too acid
stir the calcium carbonate into a little of the wine
and mix it with the main bulk and keep cool.
After the crystals of tartar have formed, syphon
off the wine without disturbing the deposit. If the
wine is not clear, fine with Bentonite (page 26).
Bottle, cork, capsule or wire and store the bottles
cool for at least three months.

Muller-Thurgau grapes (*above left*) planted at Adgestone vineyard, Isle of Wight while Lamberhurst, Kent has
the Reichensteiner (*above right*) and has been producing German style white wine since 1974 (*below*).

· GRAPE WINE 5 ·

(red, dry, table wine)

7 kg/14 lb black grapes
pectic enzyme
2 Campden tablets
wine yeast
500 g/1 lb white sugar
15 g/½ oz calcium carbonate

Crush the grapes, still on their stalks, and drop into a bin. Add the pectic enzyme and stir in the Campden tablets dissolved in a little water. (The colour is bleached a little at first but returns when fermentation begins.) Keep covered at 20–25°C/ 70–75°F. The next day add the yeast and, when fermentation starts, press down the pulp that rises to the surface in the bin. Repeat twice daily at least, until the liquid is suitably coloured.

Strain the mixture and squeeze the pulp to remove adhering liquid. Discard the residue. Add 500 g/1 lb white sugar to each 5 litres/1 gallon of liquid.

Pour the juice into a fermentation vessel. Keep at 15–20°C/60–70°F. When the frothing ceases, clean the outside of the jar and insert the air-lock. Continue to keep warm until gas bubbles no longer form.

Remove the vessel to a cold place and leave for 14 days for the wine to clear at least partially, then syphon off the wine leaving the yeast deposit behind.

If using English grapes, taste the wine to check if it is too acid. If it is too acid, stir the calcium carbonate into at little of the wine and mix it with the main bulk. Store the vessel in as cold a place as possible. Crystals of tartrate will form. Syphon

off the wine and store cool in a filled and sealed jar until the spring. Taste again. If still too acid add 5 g/½ oz BP quality potassium carbonate per 5 litres/3 gallons and again chill and syphon. Any haze in the wine can be removed by fining with Bentonite (page 26).

Dissolve one Campden tablet per 5 litres/ 1 gallon of clear wine, bottle, cork, capsule and store in a cold cellar. Serve chilled.

Heavy red wines benefit from a storage period in a clean wood cask, store (tasting each week) in new wood, longer in mature wood.

Variation

Use 2 kg/4 lb red grapes and 1 kg/2 lb white sugar or 3 kg/6 lb and ¾ kg/1½ lb respectively and the remaining ingredients and method in the recipe above. There is no need for acid reduction since the volume of juice is made up to 5 litres/1 gallon with water.

· GRAPE WINE 6 ·

(light red or white, dry, table wine)

600 ml/1 pint red or white grape juice concentrate
2 Campden tablets
900 g/1¾ lb white sugar
4 litres/6 pints water
wine yeast
nutrients
pectic enzyme (optional)

Mix the ingredients thoroughly, make up to volume with water (5 litres/1 gallon), pour into a fermentation vessel and add the yeast the next day. Hold at 20–25°C/70–75°F until the frothing ceases. Clean the outside of the jar, insert the air-lock. Keep warm until gas bubbles cease to form. Add the nutrients if fermentation is slow.

Finish as directed for a dry wine on page 44. Use the pectic enzyme if the fermented wine shows a positive reaction to the pectin test (page 151). Fine with Bentonite (page 26) if the stored wine does not clear naturally.

Variation

For a full-bodied, red or white table wine, use 1 litre/2 pints red or white grape juice concentrate, mixed with two Campden tablets and the volume made up to 5 litres/1 gallon with water. Add the yeast the next day and continue as above.

· GRAPE WINE 7 ·

(full-bodied, red, dry table wine)

1¼ litres/2 pints red grape juice concentrate
2 Campden tablets
water
wine yeast
500 g/1 lb red grapes, fresh

Mix the concentrate with the crushed Campden tablets and make up to volume with water (5 litres/1 gallon). Pour into a fermentation vessel and add the yeast the next day. Keep at 20–25°C/70–75°F until frothing ceases. Clean the outside of the jar, insert the air-lock. Keep warm until gas bubbles cease to form.

Steep the crushed, fresh red grapes in the mixture until sufficient colour has been extracted. Strain and run the coloured wine into a fermentation vessel. If necessary, make up to volume with water, insert an air-lock and keep at 20–25°C/70–75°F until gas bubbles cease to form.

Continue as directed for a dry wine on page 44.

Variation

A *dry white wine* can be made from grape concentrate using 1 kg/2 lb crushed white grapes.

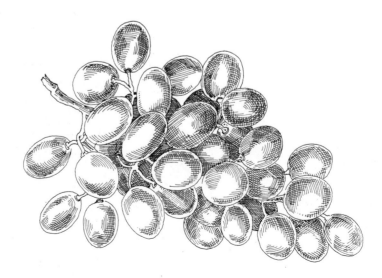

• GRAPE WINE 8 •

(rosé, dry, table wine)

1 kg/2 lb black grapes
1 kg/2 lb white grapes
pectic enzyme
2 Campden tablets
wine yeast
500 g/1 lb white sugar
15 g/½ oz calcium carbonate

Crush the grapes, still on their stalks, and drop into a bin. Add the pectic enzyme and stir in the Campden tablets dissolved in a little water. (The colour is bleached a little at first but returns when fermentation begins.) Keep at 20–25°C/70–75°F. The next day add the yeast and, when fermentation starts, press down the pulp that rises to the surface in the bin. Repeat twice daily at least until the pulp has a pleasant pink colour.

Strain the mixture and squeeze the pulp to remove adhering liquid. Discard the residue. Add 500 g/1 lb white sugar to each 5 litres/1 gallon and leave covered overnight.

Syphon off the liquid the next morning and pour the juice into a fermentation vessel. Keep at 15–20°C/60–70°F. When the frothing ceases, clean the outside of the jar and insert the air-lock. Continue to keep warm until the gas bubbles cease to form.

Remove the vessel to a cold place and leave for 14 days for the wine to clear at least partially, then syphon off the wine leaving the yeast deposit behind.

Wine from English grapes may contain too much acid. Taste to check and, if it is too acid, stir the calcium carbonate into a little of the wine and mix it with the main bulk.

Store the vessel in as cold a place as possible. Crystals of tartrate will form. Syphon off the wine and store cool in a filled and sealed jar until the spring. Taste again. If still too acid add 5 g/½ oz BP quality potassium carbonate per 5 litres/3 gallons and again chill and syphon. Any haze in the wine can be removed by fining with Bentonite (page 26).

Dissolve one Campden tablet per 5 litres/1 gallon of clear wine, bottle, cork, capsule and store in a cold cellar. If a slightly sweet flavour is required, add clear white grape juice to taste the day before drinking or use white sugar. Serve chilled.

Variation

A sweet, rosé wine can be made by increasing the amount of sugar to 1½ kg/3 lb but finishing as directed for a sweet wine on page 45.

· GRAPE WINE 9 ·

(red, sweet, dessert wine)

7 kg/14 lb black grapes

pectic enzyme

2 Campden tablets

wine yeast

500 g/1 lb white sugar

15 g/½ oz calcium carbonate

Crush the grapes, still on their stalks, and drop into a bin. Add the pectic enzyme and stir in the Campden tablets dissolved in a little water. (The colour is bleached a little at first but returns when fermentation begins.) Keep covered at 20–25°C/70–75°F. The next day add the yeast and, when fermentation starts, press down the pulp that rises to the surface in the bin. Repeat twice daily at least, until the liquid is suitably coloured.

Strain the mixture and squeeze the pulp to remove adhering liquid. Discard the residue. Add 500 g/1 lb white sugar to each 5 litres/1 gallon and leave covered overnight.

Syphon off the liquid the next morning and pour the juice into a fermentation jar and keep at 15–20°C/60–70°F. When frothing ceases, clean the outside of the jar and insert the air-lock. Continue to keep warm until the gas bubbles cease to form.

Remove the vessel to a cold place and leave for 14 days for the wine to clear at least partially, then syphon off the liquid leaving the yeast deposit behind.

Dissolve 250 g/½ lb white sugar in each 5 litres/1 gallon. Re-insert the air-lock and again keep warm at 20–25°C/70–75°F.

Continue as directed for a sweet wine on page 45. When stabilised, taste the wine. If it is too acid, deacidify by stirring calcium carbonate into a little of the wine and mixing it with the main bulk. After the crystals of tartrate have formed, syphon off the wine without disturbing the deposit. If it is not clear, fine with Bentonite (page 26). Bottle, cork, capsule or wire and store the bottles in a cool place for at least three months.

· GRAPE WINE 10 ·

(red, sweet, traditional country wine)

4 kg/8 lb red grapes

3 Campden tablets

water

pectic enzyme

1¼ kg/2½ lb white sugar

wine yeast

nutrients

15 g/½ oz calcium carbonate

Wash and drain the grapes, strip from the stalks and crush in a bowl or bin. Dissolve the Campden tablets in the water and pour over the pulp. Stir in the pectic enzyme. Leave covered with a cloth for three days, stirring frequently. Strain and dissolve the sugar in the liquid. Add the yeast and pour into a fermentation vessel, make up to volume with water if necessary (5 litres/1 gallon) and keep at 15–20°C/60–70°F. When the frothing ceases, clean the outside of the vessel and insert the air-lock. Add the nutrients if fermentation is slow. Keep warm until gas bubbles cease to form. Continue as directed for a dry wine on page 44.

When stabilised taste the wine, if it is too acid stir the calcium carbonate into a little of the wine and mix it with the main bulk. After the crystals of tartrate have formed, syphon off the wine without disturbing the deposit. If the wine is not clear, fine with Bentonite (page 26). Bottle, cork, capsule or wire and store the bottles cool for at least three months.

· GRAPE WINE 11 ·

(red or white, sweet, dessert wine)

1½ litres/2½ pints red *or* white
grape juice concentrate

---

2 Campden tablets

---

water

---

pectic enzyme

---

wine yeast

---

nutrients

Dissolve the concentrate and Campden tablets in a little water. Add the pectic enzyme, pour into fermentation vessel and make up to volume with water (5 litres/1 gallon). Add the yeast the next day. Hold at 20–25°C/70–75°F until the frothing ceases. Clean the outside of the jar, insert the air-lock. Keep warm until gas bubbles cease to form. Add the nutrients if fermentation is slow.

Continue as directed for a sweet wine on page 45.

The quality of the wine will depend upon the quality of the concentrated grape juice. Try to use red rather than red/brown and white not fawn.

Variation

Use 900 ml/1½ pints grape juice concentrate plus 500 g/1 lb white sugar and 250 g/½ lb white honey and follow the recipe above.

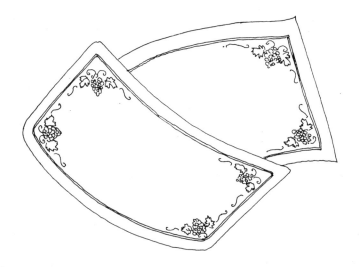

FLOWER WINES

*D*o not use protected wild flowers. The 1981 Wildlife and Country-side Act makes it illegal for anyone to uproot any wild plant in Great Britain, without authorised permission from the owner. Certain rare plants, listed in the Act, may not be picked without uprooting. Some flowers, such as primroses, not classed as rare, come under the first category and the flowers may be picked with permission. Flowers, noted chiefly for their delicate aromas, are used in making wines, either on their own, or to add distinction to other wines lacking in bouquet.

Pluck the flowers when they are fully open and dry, discarding any green calyces immediately after picking, or they will cause problems later. If the wine cannot be made soon after the flowers have been picked, lay the petals on a clean cloth in the sun to dry, or place in the oven on a low heat or in a microwave (page 20). Dried flowers, such as balm, clover, coltsfoot, cowslip, dandelion, elderflowers, lime flowers, orange blossom and wild pink rose petals can be purchased from home wine-making centres. There are also wine-making kits for elderflower and rose petal wines. The amount of *fresh* flowers to use is given in each recipe in terms of volume. Fill a jug of the required size with florets only lightly pressed down. Smaller amounts of dried flowers are needed, normally 30–60 g/1–2 oz per 5 litres/1 gallon are sufficient.

Usually the clean, dry flowers are covered with sugar syrup and yeasted. The alcohol of fermentation extracts the essential oils. It is always necessary to add citric or malic acid, or lemon or orange juice, to give the wine a crisper flavour. Some makers also add a teaspoonful of grape tannin per 5 litres/1 gallon but this is a matter for personal preference. Any lack of body can be made up by adding raisins, sultanas or concentrated white grape juice. Flower wines are very pleasant made as sparkling wines (page 48). As they are drunk the bubbles of carbon dioxide, escaping from the liquid, carry the scent of the flower to the nose of the drinker.

These wines were once drunk as much for their medicinal properties as for pleasure.

· BROOM/GORSE · WINE

(fawn, sweet, social wine)

5 litres/1 gallon broom flowers
water
2 oranges, rind and juice
2 lemons, rind and juice
2 Campden tablets
1⅓ kg/2¾ lb white sugar
nutrients
wine yeast

Strip the flowers from the shoots and put them in a muslin bag. Drop the bag in 4 litres/6 pints water with the thinly peeled fruit rinds. Bring to the boil and simmer gently for 15 minutes. Strain the liquid into a bowl or bin, squeezing out any liquid from the bag and adding it to the main bulk. Dissolve the Campden tablets, sugar and nutrients in the liquid and add the lemon and orange juices.

The next day add the yeast and keep covered at 15–20°C/60–70°F until the froth ceases to form. Pour into a fermentation vessel. Make up to volume (5 litres/1 gallon) with water, insert the air-lock and keep warm until gas bubbles no longer form.

Continue as directed for a sweet wine on page 45.

Variation

Add 245 g/8½ oz concentrated white grape juice per 5 litres/1 gallon to the combined warm liquids.

· CLOVER WINE ·

(fawn, sweet, country wine)

1⅓ kg/2¾ lb white sugar
250 g/½ lb white clover honey
water
3 Campden tablets
nutrients
5 litres/1 gallon purple clover blossoms
3 lemons, juice and rind
2 oranges, juice and rind
wine yeast

Boil the sugar, honey and 4 litres/6 pints water together for a few minutes. Take off the heat, dissolve the Campden tablets and nutrients in the syrup and pour over the flowers, fruit juices and thinly peeled rinds in a bin. Cover.

Add the yeast the next day, keep covered at 15–20°C/60–70°F for five days, stirring each day. Strain, pour the liquid into a fermentation vessel and make up to the volume with water (5 litres/1 gallon). Continue keeping warm, inserting the air-lock when frothing ceases.

Finish as directed for a sweet wine (page 45) when the gas bubbles no longer form.

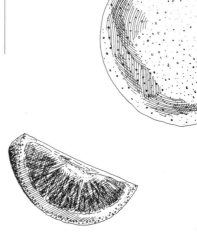

· COLTSFOOT · WINE

(fawn, sweet, social wine)

1¼ litres/2 pints coltsfoot flowers
3 oranges, juice and rind
1 lemon, juice and rind
1⅓ kg/2¾ lb white sugar
water
3 Campden tablets
nutrients
wine yeast

Snap off the full open flower heads as near to the top of the stalk as possible, or cut off with sharp scissors above the green 'button' from which the flower rises.

Wash the cut flowers in a colander and drop into a bin, add the juice and thinly peeled rind of the fruits. Pour over a hot syrup made by boiling the sugar with 4 litres/6 pints water and dissolve the Campden tablets and the nutrients in the liquid. Cover.

Add the yeast next day and leave covered for five days at 15–20°C/60–70°F stirring occasionally. Strain, pour into a fermentation vessel and make up to volume with water (5 litres/1 gallon). Continue keeping warm, inserting the air-lock when the frothing ceases.

Finish as directed for a sweet wine on page 45 when gas bubbles no longer form.

Variation

For a dry wine use 1¼ kg/2½ lb white sugar and finish as for a dry wine on page 44.

· COWSLIP WINE ·

(yellow/fawn, sweeet, country wine)

1¼ litres/2 pints cowslips
water
3 Campden tablets
1½ kg/3 lb white sugar
nutrients
10 g/⅓ oz citric or malic acid
wine yeast

Drop the flower heads, minus the green calyces, into 4 litres/6 pints water, in which the Campden tablets, sugar, nutrients and the acid have previously been dissolved. Leave overnight, then add the yeast and keep covered. The petals must be kept pressed down for a week or place them in a muslin bag and weight it down with marbles. Keep at 15–20°C/60–70°F.

Squeeze out the bag and pour the combined liquids into a fermentation vessel. Make up to volume with water (5 litres/1 gallon), insert the air-lock and continue keeping warm until gas bubbles cease to form.

Finish as directed for a sweet wine on page 45.

Variations

1. *Primroses* can be used mixed with or substituted for cowslips. The wine is richly aromatic. without being cloying.
2. The juice of an orange or lemon or 75 ml/3 fl oz pure orange juice can be substituted for the acid.
3. Add either 250 g/½ lb chopped sultanas to the petals or 245 g/8½ oz concentrated white grape juice.

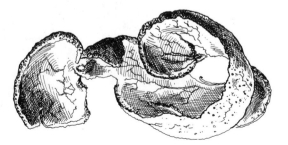

· DANDELION ·
WINE 1

(light fawn, sweet, country wine)

1¼ litres/2 pints dandelion heads
water
3 Campden tablets
1½ kg/3 lb white sugar
nutrients
10 g/⅓ oz citric or malic acid
wine yeast

Drop the flower heads, minus the green calyces, into 4 litres/6 pints water in which the Campden tablets, sugar, nutrients and the acid have previously been dissolved. Leave overnight, add the yeast, cover and keep the petals pressed down for 2 days (or contain the petals in a muslin bag weighted down with marbles). Keep at 15–20°C/60–70°F.

Squeeze out the bag and pour the combined liquids into a fermentation vessel. Make up to volume with water (5 litres/1 gallon), insert the air-lock and continue keeping warm until no more gas bubbles form.

Finish as directed for a sweet wine on page 45.

Variations

1. Use 2 litres/3 pints flower heads, 1½ kg/3 lb white sugar and four oranges instead of adding acid.
2. For a light fawn, dry table wine use 1¼ kg/2½ lb white sugar and finish as for a dry wine on page 44.
3. Substitute *pansies* for dandelions and finish as directed for a dry wine on page 44.

· DANDELION ·
WINE 2

(fawn, sweet, traditional country wine)

water
5 litres/1 gallon dandelion flowers
2 Campden tablets
2 oranges, juice and rind
2 lemons, juice and rind
1⅓ kg/2¾ lb white sugar
nutrients
wine yeast
150 ml/¼ pint brandy

Pour 4 litres/6 pints boiling water over the flower heads minus the green calyces; when cool dissolve the Campden tablets in the liquid. Leave covered for three days stirring frequently.

Strain the liquid and add it to the juice and thinly pared rind of the fruits. Add the sugar, nutrients and, when these have dissolved, the yeast. Pour into a fermentation jar and make up to volume with water (5 litres/1 gallon). Keep at 15–20°C/60–70°F, inserting an air-lock when frothing ceases. Finish as for a sweet wine on page 45 when gas bubbles no longer form.

Add the brandy when the wine is run into the final storage jar. This wine benefits from keeping.

· DANDELION ·
WINE 3

(fawn, sweet, spiced, country wine)

5 litres/1 gallon dandelion heads
water
2 Campden tablets
1 lemon, juice and rind
1 orange, juice and rind
2 kg/4 lb demerara sugar
15 g/$\frac{1}{2}$ oz root ginger
wine yeast
nutrients
250 g/$\frac{1}{2}$ lb sultanas, chopped

Put the flower heads into a bin and pour over 4 litres/6 pints boiling water. When cool dissolve the Campden tablets in the liquid and add the fruit juices. Leave covered for three days stirring several times a day.

Strain into a pan and add the sugar, thinly peeled fruit rinds and bruised ginger. Bring to the boil and simmer gently for 15 minutes. Strain again and, when cool add the yeast and nutrients. Pour back into the bin and add the sultanas. Keep covered at 15–20°C/60–70°F.

When frothing ceases, strain off the sultanas and pour the liquid into a fermentation vessel, make up to volume with water (5 litres/1 gallon) and insert the air-lock. Continue to keep warm until gas bubbles cease to form, then treat as directed for a sweet wine on page 45.

Keep the wine stored for at least a year before bottling to allow a good flavour to develop.

· ELDERFLOWER ·
WINE 1

(white, dry, table wine)

600 ml/1 pint elderflowers
2 lemons, rind and juice
1¼ kg/2½ lb white sugar
3 Campden tablets
water
nutrients
wine yeast

Gather the flower heads when they are in full bloom and when the florets are just beginning to fall. Rub the heads of the bunches together, collecting the florets in a bowl or bin. Discard the stalks. Continue until a 600 ml/1 pint jug has been filled with lightly pressed down florets.

Place the florets in a bowl or bin, add the juice and thinly peeled or grated lemon rinds, the sugar and Campden tablets. Pour over 4 litres/6 pints boiling water and stir until the sugar is dissolved.

The next day, dissolve the nutrients in the cold mixture and add the yeast. Leave for two days at 15–20°C/60–70°F, strain and pour into a fermentation vessel. Make up to volume with water (5 litres/1 gallon) and maintain the temperature until frothing ceases. Insert the air-lock and keep warm until gas bubbles no longer form.

Continue as directed for a dry wine on page 44.

Variation

Use a grapefruit instead of the lemons.

· ELDERFLOWER ·
WINE 2

(light fawn, sweet, social wine)

600 ml/1 pint elderflowers
water
2 Campden tablets
2 oranges, juice and rind
1¼ kg/2½ lb white sugar
wine yeast
nutrients
500 g/1 lb sultanas, chopped

Rub the flower heads together and then place the florets in a bowl or bin and pour over 4 litres/6 pints boiling water. When cool dissolve the Campden tablets in the liquid and add the fruit juice. Leave covered for three days stirring several times a day.

Strain into a pan and add the sugar and thinly peeled fruit rind. Bring to the boil and simmer gently for 15 minutes. Strain again and, when cool add the yeast and nutrients. Pour back into the bin and add the sultanas. Keep covered at 15–20°C/60–70°F. When frothing ceases, strain off the sultanas and pour the liquid into a fermentation vessel, make up to volume with water (5 litres/1 gallon) and insert the air-lock when frothing ceases. Continue to keep warm until gas bubbles no longer form, then treat as directed for a sweet wine on page 45.

Variations

1. Substitute six mandarins, tangerines or satumas for the oranges.
2. Substitute concentrated white grape juice (490 g/17 oz) for the sultanas.

· ELDERFLOWER ·
WINE 3

(white, semi-sparkling, traditional summer drink)

2 heads elderflowers
1 lemon, juice and rind
750 g/1½ lb white sugar
60 ml/2 fl oz white wine vinegar
water

Rub bunches of elderflower heads together and place the florets in a bowl or bin, followed by the lemon juice, thinly peeled and cut up rind, sugar and vinegar. Add cold water to make up the volume (5 litres/1 gallon) and stir to dissolve the sugar. Leave covered for 24 hours.

Strain into strong screw-topped or heavy champagne bottles. Leave for two weeks at 20°C/70°F when this summer drink should be semi-sparkling and ready to drink.

The yeast that produced the carbon dioxide gas is a weakly fermenting species, derived from the flowers. Hence, Campden tablets, wine yeast and nutrients are not added to the mixture. Consequently in some years the product may develop an oily texture due to the action of certain types of lactic acid bacteria. Their action can be restricted by using the correct strength and amount of vinegar, by substituting glucose for white sugar and by keeping the fermentation temperature above 15°C/60°F.

· GOLDEN ROD ·
WINE

(light fawn, sweet, country wine)

1½ kg/3 lb white sugar
water
600 ml/1 pint golden rod blossoms
6 sweet oranges, juice and rind
2 Campden tablets
wine yeast
nutrients
250 g/½ lb sultanas, chopped

Simmer the sugar and 4 litres/6 pints water together for a few minutes to allow the sugar to dissolve. Pour the boiling syrup on to the blossoms, orange juice, grated rind and crushed Campden tablets. Stir to mix.

The next day add the yeast, nutrients and chopped sultanas. Keep covered at 15–20°C/60–70°F for five days, stirring daily. Strain, pour the liquid into a fermentation vessel and make up to volume with water (5 litres/1 gallon). Keep warm until frothing ceases, insert the air-lock and continue keeping warm until gas bubbles no longer form.

Continue as directed for a sweet wine on page 45.

Variation

Substitute 1 litre/2 pints *hawthorn* (May) blossoms for those of the golden rod. Use three Campden tablets, not two and one orange not six.

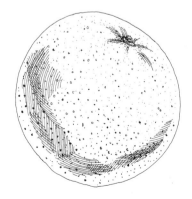

· HAWTHORN ·
FLOWER WINE
(light fawn, sweet, country wine)

1½ kg/3 lb white sugar
2 lemons, rind and juice
water
nutrients
2 Campden tablets
wine yeast
2½ litres/4 pints hawthorn flowers

Simmer the sugar and grated lemon rinds in 4 litres/6 pints water for 15 minutes. Pour through a strainer into a bin, add the lemon juice and dissolve the nutrients and Campden tablets in the liquid. The next day add the yeast and the flowers. Cover, keep at 15–20°C/60–70°F for another eight days, stirring each day.

Strain, pour the liquid into a fermentation vessel, make up to volume with water (5 litres/1 gallon) and continue keeping warm. Insert the air-lock when frothing ceases. Continue as directed for a sweet wine on page 45.

· MARIGOLD ·
WINE
(yellow fawn, sweet, country wine)

1½ kg/3 lb white sugar
water
5 litres/1 gallon marigold petals
3 Campden tablets
nutrients
2 lemons, juice and rind
wine yeast

Simmer the sugar and 4 litres/6 pints water together for a few minutes to dissolve and then allow to cool. Add the petals, crushed Campden tablets, nutrients, lemon juice and thinly peeled rinds. Stir to dissolve the soluble ingredients.

Add the yeast the next day, leave covered for four days at 15–20°C/60–70°F, stirring twice daily. Strain, pour into a fermentation vessel, make up to volume with water (5 litres/1 gallon) and continue to keep warm. Insert an air-lock when frothing ceases. Continue as directed for a sweet wine on page 45 when gas bubbles cease to form.

· PANSY WINE ·

(fawn, sweet, country wine)

10 litres/2 gallons pansies
15 g/½ oz ginger powder
2 Campden tablets
2 lemons, juice and rind
2 oranges, juice and rind
2 large sweet apples
pectic enzyme
1½ kg/3 lb white sugar
nutrients
water
wine yeast

Lay the fresh-picked, white or purple, pansy flowers on a clean cloth in the warm sun for three days to dry. Put alternate layers of dried pansies in a bowl or bin and dust with ginger powder and the crushed Campden tablets. Leave covered for three days, stirring and mashing each day.

Add the juice and thinly peeled rinds of the oranges and lemons and the thinly sliced apples. Add the pectic enzyme, sugar and nutrients, 4 litres/6 pints lukewarm water and the yeast. Leave covered for three days at 15–20°C/60–70°F, stirring vigorously twice daily.

Strain, pour into a fermentaion vessel, make up to volume with water (5 litres/1 gallon) and continue to keep warm. Insert an air-lock when frothing ceases and continue as directed for a sweet wine on page 45 when gas bubbles no longer form.

Variation

Reduce the amount of flowers to 2½ litres/4 pints and omit the ginger and lemons.

· ROSE PETAL · WINE 1

(rosé, sweet, social wine)

1 kg/2 lb white sugar
water
4 litres/6 pints scented rose petals
nutrients
3 Campden tablets
1 orange, juice
1 lemon, juice
wine yeast

Dissolve the sugar in 4 litres/6 pints water and pour into a bowl or bin containing the freshly picked or frozen rose petals, nutrients and the crushed Campden tablets. Stir to dissolve and add the fruit juices (no skin).

Add the yeast the next day and cover, keep at 15–20°C/60–70°F, stirring once a day for nine days. Strain, pour the liquid into a fermentation vessel, make up to volume with water (5 litres/1 gallon) and continue to keep warm. Insert the air-lock when frothing ceases and continue as directed for a sweet wine on page 45 when gas bubbles no longer form.

When making Rose Petal Wine, use only the strongest scented roses. The old-fashioned, heavily scented varieties, such as the China Rose, Damask or Musk Rose are best, but don't forget Fragrant Cloud and similarly scented modern roses. As few gardeners have sufficient of these roses to find a gallon of petals, the amount of blossoms can be reduced to 1¼ litres/2 pints to make a more delicate flavoured wine or use air or microwave-dried petals.

There is a wine-making kit for making rose petal wine.

· ROSE PETAL ·
WINE 2
(rosé, dry, table wine)

600 ml/1 pint rose petals
water
3 Campden tablets
1 kg/2 lb white sugar
nutrients
245 g/8½ oz concentrated white grape juice
10g/⅓ oz malic acid
wine yeast

Drop the petals into 4 litres/6 pints water, in which the Campden tablets, sugar, nutrients, grape concentrate and the acid have previously been dissolved.

Leave overnight, add the yeast and keep covered. The petals must be kept pressed down for a week (or contain the petals in a muslin bag weighted down with marbles). Keep at 15–20°C/60–70°F.

Squeeze out the bag and pour the combined liquids into a fermentation vessel. Make up to volume with water (5 litres/1 gallon), insert the air-lock and continue keeping warm until gas bubbles cease to form. Continue as for a dry wine on page 44.

The colour of the wine will depend on the colour of the petals.

· WALLFLOWER ·
WINE
(fawn, dry, table wine)

1 kg/2 lb white sugar
2 Campden tablets
water
600 ml/1 pint wallflower blossoms
90 ml/3 fl oz orange juice
245 g/8½ oz concentrated white grape juice
pectic enzyme
nutrients
wine yeast

Dissolve the sugar and the Campden tablets in 4 litres/6 pints boiling water and pour over the blossoms. When cool, stir in the orange juice, grape concentrate, pectic enzyme and nutrients. Cover.

Add the yeast the next day, keep covered at 15–20°C/60–70°F for three days. Strain, pour into a fermentation vessel, make up to volume with water (5 litres/1 gallon) and insert the air-lock when frothing ceases.

Continue as directed for a dry wine on page 44 when gas bubbles no longer form.

Above: A wide variety of dried flowers can be used to produce wine if fresh flowers are not in bloom.

HERB WINES
(including Ginger Wines)

Herb wines were once made as much for their medicinal properties as for their pleasant flavours. Those most frequently used for wine-making are agrimony, balm, ginger, nettle, parsley and tea. The method of preparation is given with each recipe and consists mainly of making an extract by pouring boiling water over the leafy material or simmering it in water. Wines can also be made by steeping the material in a plain white dry or sweet wine (pages 44 and 45).

There are now many more herbs available as seeds, plants or dried material. They can be used as a base for wines, but try them first on a small scale. The wines should be considered not only for table or social wines, but also as aperitifs.

The amount of fresh herbs to use is given in nearly every recipe by volume. Fill a jug of the required size with the herbs and press down lightly. If using dried herbs refer to Raw Materials (page 19).

Herbs that might be considered for wines or have been used for these purposes in the past, are as follows:

Angelica. Reminiscent of muscat grapes. The flavour comes from the entire plant and has been used to give a muscat character to other wines.

Balm. Infuse in dry or sweet raisin wine.

Bergamot. Aromatic dried leaves, sometimes used in herb teas. The leaves and flowers retain their fragrance on drying. Heat in punches and fruit drinks.

Borage. Cucumber flavour. One or two leaves used to flavour wines and cold cups.

Salad Burnet. Steep in wine.

Camomile. Apple flavour. Used in the making of some vermouths and light wines and also as a tea.

Caraway Seeds. Try adding to wine.

Cardamon. Use fresh ground seeds. Bitter-sweet and slightly lemony.

Carnation. Really the clove scented pink. Use the coloured parts of the petals only.

The flavour of most herb wines is extracted by pouring boiling water over the leafy material or simmering it in water.

Clove. Infuse the crushed cloves in orange wine and use a basis for a liqueur.

Coriander Seeds. These are one of the ingredients used in making gin. Sweet and savoury. The oil from the crushed seeds is used in some cordials.

Dill. Mild, sweet, caraway type flavour.

Fennel and French Tarragon. They have a strong aniseed flavour. Sweet Cicely also has a slight aniseed taste.

Geranium (scented). Leaves used in fruit punches.

Juniper. Seeds take a long time to ripen. One of the main flavour components of gin. An aperitif can be made by soaking the dried berries in wine.

Lemon Thyme. Delicate lemon flavour.

Lemon Verbena. Steep leaves in drinks when a strong lemon flavour is required.

Mint. Eau-de-Cologne variety used in citrus drinks. Also try apple and pineapple mints in wine.

Mugwort. Oil used in vermouth.

Rosemary. Distinctive, delicate, sweetish flavour, something like a lemony sage.

· AGRIMONY ·
WINE

(fawn, medium sweet, spiced, social wine)

1¼ litres/2 pints agrimony leaves
60 g/2 oz root ginger
water
3 oranges, rind and juice
3 lemons, rind and juice
2 Campden tablets
1½ kg/3 lb white or brown sugar
nutrients
250 g/½ lb sultanas *or* 250 g/8½ oz concentrated white grape juice
wine yeast

Gather the leaves in July. They can be used fresh or dried (half the quantity). Simmer the washed leaves and crushed ginger in 4 litres/6 pints water until a good colour is obtained, adding more water, if necessary to maintain the volume.

Strain and pour the hot liquid on to the thinly peeled rinds and the juice of the citrus fruits in a bowl or bin. Dissolve the Campden tablets, sugar and nutrients in the liquid. Add the chopped sultanas or concentrate. Add the yeast the next day. Keep covered at about 20°C/70°F for three days, stirring twice a day. Strain and pour the liquid into a fermentation vessel. Make up to volume with water (5 litres/1 gallon) and continue keeping warm. When frothing ceases, insert the air-lock and, when gas bubbles no longer form, continue as for a sweet wine on page 45.

Variation

Substitute 10 g/⅓ oz citric or malic acid for the oranges and lemons.

· BALM WINE ·

(fawn, sweet, country wine)

2½ litres/4 pints balm or lemon scented balm leaves
1½ kg/3 lb white sugar
2 lemons, rind and juice
water
3 Campden tablets
nutrients
wine yeast

Wash the leaves and young shoots or use a small packet of the dried material. Simmer the sugar, thinly peeled lemon rinds and 4 litres/6 pints water together for 15 minutes. Pour over the balm leaves and shoots, dissolving the Campden tablets and nutrients in the liquid. When cool add the lemon juice and, next day, the yeast.

Leave covered at about 20°C/70°F for four days, stirring twice daily. Strain, pour the liquid into a fermentation vessel and make up to volume with water (5 litres/1 gallon). Keep warm, insert the air-lock when frothing ceases.

Continue as directed for a sweet wine on page 45 when gas bubbles no longer form.

Variation

Sultanas (250 g/½ lb) or concentrated white grape juice (250 g/8½ oz) can be added before the yeast.

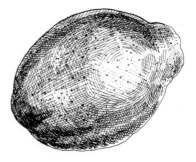

· GINGER WINE 1 ·

(fawn, sweet, dessert wine)

60 g/2 oz dried root ginger
250 g/½ lb raisins, chopped
2 oranges, rind and juice
2 lemons, rind and juice
water
2 Campden tablets
1½ kg/3 lb demerara sugar
nutrients
wine yeast

Simmer the bruised ginger, raisins and thinly peeled orange and lemon rinds for 15 minutes in 1 litre/2 pints water. Strain off the liquid and reserve. Treat the pulp with another 1 litre/2 pints boiling water. Repeat once more and combine the three batches of liquid. Add the fruit juices and dissolve the Campden tablets, sugar and nutrients in the liquid.

Add the yeast the next day, pour into a fermentation vessel and make up to volume with water (5 litres/1 gallon). Keep at about 20°C/70°F inserting the air-lock when frothing ceases. When gas bubbles no longer form, continue as directed for a sweet wine on page 45.

The amount of dried ginger in this recipe does not give an obtrusive flavour, but it should be altered to suit individual palates.

Variation

Substitute 250 ml/½ pint pure orange juice, for the citrus fruit and add the pectic enzyme with the Campden tablets.

· GINGER WINE 2 ·

(fawn, sweet, country wine)

30 g/1 oz hops (dried)
2 oranges, rind and juice
60 g/2 oz root ginger
water
1½ kg/3 lb white sugar
3 Campden tablets
nutrients
wine yeast

Simmer the hops, thinly peeled orange rinds and crushed ginger in 4 litres/6 pints water for 20 minutes. Strain and pour the liquid over the sugar, Campden tablets, nutrients and orange juice. Stir to dissolve.

Add the yeast the next day, pour into a fermentation vessel and make up to volume with water (5 litres/1 gallon). Keep at about 20°C/70°F, inserting the air-lock when frothing ceases.

When the gas bubbles no longer form continue as directed for a sweet wine on page 45.

Variation

Another slightly bitter-sweet aperitif type wine can be made by omitting the hops and substituting three Seville oranges for the two sweet oranges.

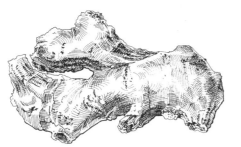

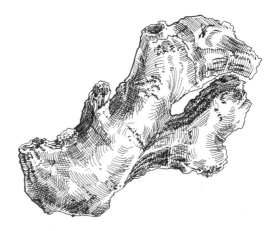

· NETTLE WINE ·

(pale gold, dry, country wine)

2½ litres/4 pints nettles
water
15 g/½ oz root ginger
2 oranges *or* lemons, rind and juice
1¼ kg/2½ lb white sugar
3 Campden tablets
nutrients
wine yeast

Collect young nettle tops in the late spring, wash in a colander and drain. Drop into 4 litres/6 pints boiling water, together with the bruised ginger and thinly peeled orange or lemon rinds. Simmer gently for 20 minutes. Strain the mixture on to the sugar, Campden tablets, nutrients and fruit juice in a bowl or bin. Mix to dissolve.

Add the yeast the next day, pour into a fermentation vessel and make up to volume with water (5 litres/1 gallon). Keep at about 20°C/70°F, inserting the air-lock when frothing ceases. When gas bubbles no longer form, continue as directed for a dry wine on page 44.

Variations

1. Omit the ginger and/or add 245 g/8½ oz concentrated white grape juice.
2. Substitute brown sugar for the white, and finish as directed for a sweet wine on page 45.

· PARSLEY WINE 1 ·

(fawn, sweet, country wine)

500 g/1 lb parsley heads
2 oranges, rind and juice
2 lemons, rind and juice
water
2 kg/4 lb demerara sugar
2 Campden tablets
nutrients
pectic enzyme
wine yeast

Pluck the parsley heads from the stalks before weighing. Wash well, drain and place in a bowl or bin with the thinly peeled orange and lemon rinds. Pour on 4 litres/6 pints boiling water and strain after 24 hours. Alternatively, put the ingredients in a muslin bag and suspend in the simmering water for 15 minutes. Strain when cool.

Dissolve the sugar and Campden tablets in the liquid, add the fruit juices, nutrients, and stir in the pectic enzyme. Add the yeast the next day, pour into a fermentation vessel and make up to volume with water (5 litres/1 gallon). Keep at about 20°C/70°F, inserting the air-lock when frothing ceases. When gas bubbles no longer form, continue as directed for a sweet wine on page 45.

Variations

1. Substitute 1½ kg/3 lb white sugar for the demerara.
2. Add 30 g/1 oz crushed ginger root with the parsley heads and citrus peel.

· PARSLEY WINE 2 ·

(fawn, sweet, country wine)

375 g/¾ lb parsley heads
water
30 g/1 oz root ginger
2 lemons, rind and juice
1½ kg/3 lb white sugar
3 Campden tablets
nutrients
wine yeast

Collect the parsley heads and wash in a colander then drain. Drop into 4 litres/6 pints boiling water, together with the bruised ginger and thinly peeled lemon rinds. Simmer gently for 20 minutes. Strain the mixture on to the sugar, Campden tablets, nutrients and fruit juice in a bowl or bin. Mix to dissolve.

Add the yeast the next day, pour into a fermentation vessel and make up to volume with water (5 litres/1 gallon). Keep at about 20°C/70°F, inserting the air-lock when frothing ceases. When gas bubbles no longer form, continue as directed for a sweet wine on page 45.

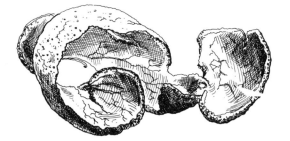

· PARSLEY WINE 3 ·

(fawn, sweet, country wine)

500 g/1 lb parsley heads
60 g/2 oz tender fresh herb (balm, comfrey, rosemary etc.)
60 g/2 oz mint shoots
water
30 g/1 oz root ginger
1 lemon, rind and juice
1½ kg/3 lb white sugar
nutrients
3 Campden tablets
wine yeast

Wash and drain all the herbs and place in a large saucepan with 4 litres/6 pints water, the bruised ginger and the thinly peeled lemon rind. Simmer for 30 minutes, then pour the strained liquid over the lemon juice, sugar, nutrients and Campden tablets. Stir to dissolve.

Add the yeast the next day, pour into a fermentation vessel and make up to volume with water (5 litres/1 gallon). Keep at about 20°C/70°F, inserting the air-lock when frothing ceases. When gas bubbles no longer form, continue as directed for a sweet wine on page 45.

· PARSLEY WINE 4 ·

(fawn, dry, table wine)

375 g/¾ lb parsley heads
250 g/½ lb sultanas, chopped
water
200 ml/⅓ pint pure orange juice
2 Campden tablets
1 kg/2 lb white sugar
pectic enzyme
nutrients
wine yeast

Pluck the parsley heads from the stalks, weigh, wash and drain. Place in a bowl or bin with the sultanas. Pour on 4 litres/6 pints boiling water. Leave until cool and add the orange juice and Campden tablets dissolved in a little hot water. Stir and cover.

Twenty-four hours later, strain on to the sugar, pectic enzyme and nutrients. Stir to dissolve. Add the yeast the next day, pour into a fermentation vessel and make up to volume with water (5 litres/1 gallon). Keep at about 20°C/70°F inserting the air-lock when frothing ceases. When gas bubbles no longer form continue as directed for a dry wine on page 44.

· ROSEMARY ·
WINE

(fawn, sweet, social wine)

70 g/2½ oz young rosemary shoots
750 ml/26 fl oz neutral sweet wine

Bruise and soak the rosemary shoots in the wine until it has the required flavour. Strain and run the wine into a bottle and insert an air-lock. Keep warm (20°C/70°F) for 3 weeks to ensure the wine is stable against refermentation (if not follow the directions on page 46). Replace the air-lock with a cork and store for three months before drinking.

· TEA WINE 1 ·

(fawn, dry, table wine)

4 litres/6 pints tea extract
1¼ kg/2½ lb white sugar
3 Campden tablets
nutrients
2 lemons, juice and rind
wine yeast
water

Use fresh tea made to normal strength. Ceylon and Indian teas give full-bodied wines. If necessary, this can be reduced by pouring the first extract for cups of tea, then filling the pot with a fresh charge of water, letting it stand five minutes, then using this extract to make the wine. Teas such as Earl Grey and the milder flavoured China teas also make very pleasant wines. Tea extract is sometimes used as an alternative to dried grape tannin in recipes for other wines where there is a noticeable lack of astringency or the flavour 'disappears' quickly after tasting.

Add the hot tea to a bowl or bin containing the sugar, Campden tablets, nutrients and the juice and grated rind of the lemons. Leave overnight and strain, adding the yeast the next day. Pour into a fermentation vessel and make up to volume with water (5 litres/1 gallon). Keep at about 20°C/70°F, inserting the air-lock when frothing ceases. When gas bubbles cease to form, continue as directed for a dry wine on page 44.

· TEA WINE 2 ·

(fawn, sweet, social wine)

4 litres/6 pints tea extract
250 g/½ lb raisins *or* sultanas
3 Campden tablets
200 ml/⅓ pint pure orange juice
1½ kg/3 lb white sugar
nutrients
wine yeast
water

Pour 4 litres/6 pints hot tea on to the chopped raisins and crushed Campden tablets in a bowl or bin. When cool, stir in the orange juice and cover. Leave for three days, stirring twice daily. Strain into a fermentation vessel and add the sugar and nutrients. Shake or stir to dissolve.

Add the yeast the next day, pour into a fermentation vessel and make up to volume with water (5 litres/1 gallon). Keep at about 20°C/70°F, inserting the air-lock when frothing ceases. When gas bubbles no longer form, continue as directed for a sweet wine on page 45.

VEGETABLE
WINES

Rhubarb is included in this chapter although handbooks on canning and bottling include it amongst fruits, because of its acidity. Squash and pumpkin are included because the method of wine-making is the same as for Marrow Wine.

Parsnips and rhubarb make excellent wines on their own. Beetroot should be stored long enough for the slightly earthy taste to disappear. Most of the other vegetables make rather bland wines and need the addition of fresh or dried fruits and/or spices.

In general, old root vegetables are used. They are scrubbed clean, diced and boiled, without a lid on the saucepan, until *just* tender. The extract can be used for wine-making and the diced vegetables can be cooked a little more and eaten as usual.

The potato/raisin group of wines are probably the most traditional. Some of the recipes include grains, such as wheat, barley and rice. These contribute little to the alcohol content, unless malted previously or treated with a starch destroying enzyme. They probably help the wine to clear and add a little to the flavour.

· BEETROOT ·
WINE 1

(light red, dry, table wine)

2½ kg/5 lb old beetroot
water
1 lemon, rind and juice
1¼ kg/2½ lb white sugar
3 Campden tablets
nutrients
pectic enzyme
wine yeast

Cut off and discard the leafy tops and then wash the beetroot. Cut up into small cubes, and drop directly into 4 litres/6 pints cold water with the grated lemon rind. Boil until tender and then strain. Discard the pulp. Dissolve the sugar, Campden tablets and nutrients in the hot liquid. When the liquid is cool, add the lemon juice and stir in the pectic enzyme. Cover.

The next day add the yeast, pour into a fermentation vessel, make up to volume with water (5 litres/1 gallon) and keep at 20–25°C/70–75°F. Insert the air-lock when frothing ceases and continue as directed for a dry wine on page 44 when gas bubbles no longer form.

The colour of the wine can change during prolonged storage to fawn/red due to precipitation of some of the colouring matter. This change can be diminished by keeping vessels and bottles of wine in the dark.

Variations

1. Replace the lemon with 15 g/½ oz citric or malic acid and add with the Campden tablets.
2. For a red, sweet, country beetroot wine increase the sugar to 1½ kg/3 lb per 5 litres/ 1 gallon and use an orange instead of a lemon.

· BEETROOT ·
WINE 2

(red, sweet, spiced, country wine)

2 kg/4 lb old beetroot
water
4 cloves
15 g/½ oz root ginger
3 Campden tablets
1½ kg/3 lb white sugar
nutrients
60 ml/2 fl oz orange juice
pectic enzyme
wine yeast

Discard the leafy tops of the beetroot. Wash the roots well and slice into 4 litres/6 pints cold water. Boil with the cloves and crushed ginger until the slices are tender. Strain the hot liquid into a bowl or bin containing the crushed Campden tablets, sugar and nutrients. Stir to dissolve. When the liquid is cool add the fruit juice and the pectic enzyme. Cover.

The next day add the yeast, pour into a fermentation vessel and make up to volume with water (5 litres/1 gallon) and keep at 20–25°C/70–75°F. Insert the air-lock when frothing ceases.

Continue as directed for a sweet wine on page 45 when gas bubbles no longer form.

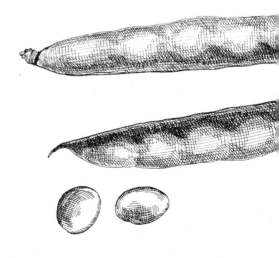

· BROAD BEAN ·
WINE

(fawn, dry, table wine)

2 kg/4 lb broad beans (shelled)
water
245 g/8½ oz concentrated white grape juice
3 Campden tablets
1¼ kg/2½ lb white sugar
nutrients
15 g/½ oz citric or malic acid
pectic enzyme
wine yeast

Use old broad beans. Discard the shells and simmer the beans slowly with the lid off the saucepan in 4 litres/6 pints water until tender but before the skins break. Strain and run the hot liquid on to the concentrate, crushed Campden tablets, sugar, nutrients and acid. When cool, stir in the pectic enzyme and cover.

The next day add the yeast, pour into a fermentation vessel, make up to volume with water (5 litres/1 gallon) and keep at 15–20°C/60–70°F. Insert the air-lock when frothing ceases.

Continue as directed for a dry wine on page 44 when gas bubbles no longer form.

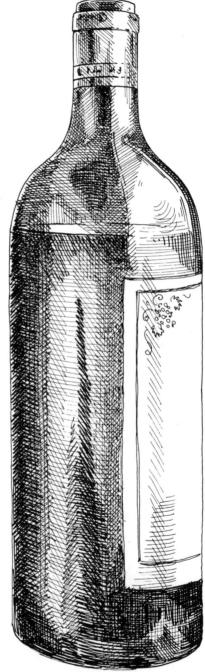

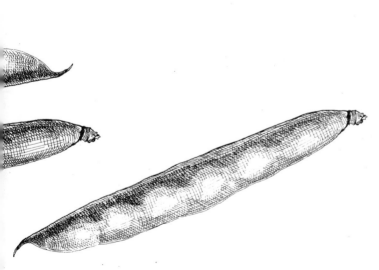

· CARROT WINE 1 ·

(fawn, sweet, dessert wine)

2 kg/4 lb carrots
water
245 g/8¼ oz concentrated white grape juice
3 Campden tablets
1½ kg/3 lb white sugar
nutrients
15 g/½ oz citric or malic acid
pectic enzyme
wine yeast

Discard the leafy tops. Wash the carrots well and slice into 4 litres/6 pints cold water and simmer until the slices are tender. Strain and run the hot liquid into a bowl or bin containing the concentrate, the crushed Campden tablets, sugar, nutrients and acid. Stir to dissolve. When the liquid is cool, add the pectic enzyme. Cover.

The next day add the yeast, pour into a fermentation vessel, make up to volume with water (5 litres/1 gallon) and keep at 20–25°C/70–75°F. Insert the air-lock when frothing ceases and continue as directed for a sweet wine on page 45 when gas bubbles no longer form.

Variation

Substitute *parsnips* for carrots.

· CARROT WINE 2 ·

(fawn, sweet, spiced, country wine)

2 kg/4 lb carrots
water
60 g/2 oz root ginger
250 g/½ lb raisins, chopped
3 Campden tablets
2 kg/4 lb demerara sugar
nutrients
pectic enzyme
2 oranges, juice
2 lemons, juice
wine yeast

Scrub the carrots clean and slice into 4 litres/6 pints cold water. Drop in the crushed ginger root and simmer until the slices are just tender. Strain the boiling liquid into a bowl or bin containing the raisins, crushed Campden tablets, sugar and nutrients. Stir to dissolve. When cool add the pectic enzyme and the fruit juices; cover. Add the yeast the next day and keep covered at 20–25°C/70–75°F for three days, stirring twice daily.

Strain into a fermentation vessel and make up to volume with water (5 litres/1 gallon) and keep warm. Insert the air-lock when frothing ceases and finish off as directed for a sweet wine on page 45 when gas bubbles no longer form.

Variations

1. Use 1 kg/2 lb each of white and demerara sugar.
2. The root ginger can be omitted if a spiced wine is not wanted.
3. Pure carrot juice, and carrot and apple juice, can now be purchased canned or bottled. Use 1¼ litres/2 pints instead of the specified weight of roots.
4. Substitute *parsnips* for the carrots in the above recipe.

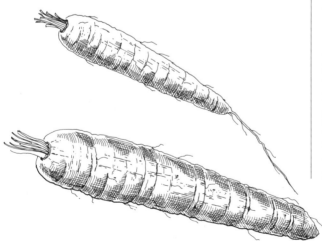

· CELERY WINE ·

(light fawn, sweet, social wine or aperitif)

2 kg/4 lb celery
water
245 g/8¼ oz concentrated white grape juice
3 Campden tablets
1⅓ kg/2¾ lb white sugar
nutrients
15 g/½ oz citric or malic acid
pectic enzyme
wine yeast

Cut off and discard the green leaves and the roots of the celery. Scrub the stalks well and cut into short lengths, dropping them into 4 litres/6 pints boiling water. Simmer until the sections are just tender. Strain the liquid into a bowl or bin containing the concentrate, crushed Campden tablets, sugar, nutrients and acid. Stir to dissolve. When cool stir in the pectic enzyme.

The next day pour into the fermentation vessel, add the yeast and make up to volume with water (5 litres/1 gallon). Keep at 15–20°C/60–70°F, inserting the air-lock when frothing ceases.

Continue as directed for a sweet wine on page 45 when the gas bubbles no longer form.

Variation

Celeriac or root celery, resembling a rough-skinned turnip, has a celery flavour and might be tried using the same recipe. Discard any green tops and scrub the roots clean and slice.

· LETTUCE WINE ·

(fawn, sweet, country wine)

500 g/1 lb wheat
water
1½ kg/3 lb lettuce
250 g/½ lb raisins *or* sultanas
3 Campden tablets
1¼ kg/2½ lb white sugar
nutrients
1 orange
1 lemon
pectic enzyme
wine yeast

Place the wheat in water 24 hours before making the wine. Remove the roots of the lettuce and the central 'milky' stalk. Simmer the chopped leaves in 4 litres/6 pints water, then strain the liquid into a bowl or bin containing the drained and minced wheat (discard the soaking water), chopped raisins, crushed Campden tablets, sugar, nutrients and thinly sliced citrus fruits. Stir to dissolve the soluble ingredients. When cool stir in the pectic enzyme and leave covered overnight.

Add the yeast the next day and keep covered at 15–20°C/60–70°F for seven days, stirring twice daily. Strain the liquid into a fermentation vessel, make up to volume with water (5 litres/1 gallon) and keep warm. Insert the air-lock when frothing ceases.

Continue as directed for a sweet wine on page 45 when the gas bubbles no longer form.

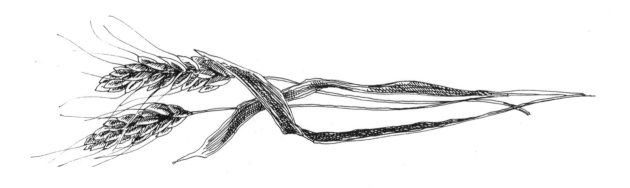

· MANGOLD WINE ·

(fawn, sweet, country wine)

2 kg/4 lb mangolds
water
30 g/1 oz hops
1 orange, rind and juice
1 lemon, rind and juice
3 Campden tablets
1½ kg/3 lb demerara sugar
nutrients
pectic enzyme
wine yeast

Scrub the roots clean and slice into a saucepan. Add 4 litres/6 pints water and suspend the hops in a muslin bag in the pan. Boil until the slices are tender then strain. Discard the hops. Resuspend the bag, this time containing the thinly peeled orange and lemon rinds, in the liquid and simmer again for 20 minutes. Remove the bag and pour the liquid into a bowl or bin containing the crushed Campden tablets, sugar, nutrients and fruit juices. Stir to dissolve and add the pectic enzyme when cool. Cover.

The next day add the yeast, pour into a fermentation vessel, make up to volume with water (5 litres/1 gallon) and keep at 20–25°C/70–75°F. Insert the air-lock when frothing ceases. Continue as directed for a sweet wine on page 45 when the gas bubbles no longer form.

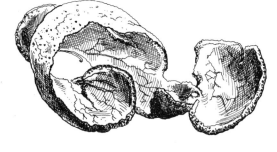

· MARROW WINE ·

(fawn, sweet, country wine)

2 kg/4 lb ripe marrow
3 Campden tablets
1½ kg/3 lb white sugar
nutrients
2 oranges
2 lemons
water
pectic enzyme
wine yeast

Peel the marrow and dice the pulp and seeds into a bowl or bin. Add the crushed Campden tablets, sugar, nutrients and sliced oranges and lemons. Pour over 4 litres/6 pints boiling water and stir to dissolve the soluble ingredients.

When cool stir in the pectic enzyme and cover. The next day add the yeast and keep covered at 15–20°C/60–70°F for five days, stirring frequently.

Strain into the fermentation vessel, make up to volume with water (5 litres/1 gallon) and keep warm. Insert the air-lock when frothing ceases and continue as directed for a sweet wine on page 45 when the gas bubbles no longer form.

Variation

1. Substitute 1 kg/2 lb white honey and 1 kg/2 lb white sugar or 2 kg/4 lb demerara sugar for the white sugar.
2. A spiced wine can be made by adding 30 g/1 oz crushed ginger root in the initial water and simmering for 15 minutes before pouring on to the other ingredients in the bowl or bin.
3. The following substitutes for marrows can be used: *pumpkin* (but not seed or fibre), *courgettes*, *tindoori*, *squashes* (golden nugget – peeled, custard and butternut) and *sugarbeet*.

· PARSNIP WINE 1 ·

(white, dry, table wine)

1½ kg/3 lb parsnips
water
1¼ kg/2½ lb white sugar
3 Campden tablets
nutrients
10 g/⅓ oz citric or malic acid
pectic enzyme
wine yeast

Use mild flavoured varieties of parsnips, stored outside until any starch has been converted to sugar. Starchy parsnips may need the addition of both starch destroying and pectic enzymes to the extract.

Scrub the roots well, cut out scabs but do not peel (unless it is intended to eat the vegetable afterwards), cube or slice and drop into 4 litres/6 pints boiling water. Simmer gently and strain as soon as a fork can be pushed into the cubes or slices. Do *not* let the parsnips become mushy and do not squeeze the cooked cubes when straining them. Run the strained liquid into a bowl or bin containing the sugar, crushed Campden tablets, nutrients and acid. When cool stir in the pectic enzyme.

The next day pour the liquid into a fermentation vessel, add the yeast and make up to volume with water (5 litres/1 gallon). Keep at 15–20°C/60–70°F, inserting the air-lock when frothing ceases.

Continue as directed for a dry wine on page 44 when the gas bubbles no longer form.

Variation

Add the grated rind of two oranges with the parsnip cubes and the juice with the pectic enzyme.

· PARSNIP WINE 2 ·

(fawn, sweet, country wine)

2 kg/4 lb parsnips
water
250 g/½ lb raisins *or* sultanas, chopped
3 Campden tablets
1¼ kg/2½ lb white sugar
nutrients
pectic enzyme
125 ml/4 fl oz pure orange juice
wine yeast

Scrub the parsnips clean and slice into 4 litres/6 pints cold water. Simmer until the slices are just tender. Strain the boiling liquid into a bowl or bin containing the raisins, crushed Campden tablets, sugar and nutrients. Stir to dissolve.

When cool add the pectic enzyme and the fruit juice; cover. Add the yeast the next day and keep covered at 20–25°C/70–75°F for three days, stirring twice daily.

Strain into the fermentation vessel and make up to volume with water (5 litres/1 gallon) and keep warm. Insert the air-lock when frothing ceases and finish off as directed for a sweet wine on page 45 when the gas bubbles no longer form.

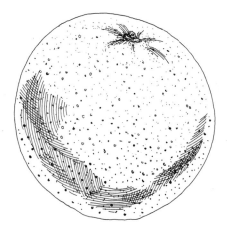

· PARSNIP & ·
BEETROOT WINE

(red, sweet, spiced, country wine)

1½ kg/3 lb old beetroot
1 kg/2 lb frosted parsnips
water
4 cloves
15 g/½ oz root ginger
3 Campden tablets
1½ kg/3 lb white sugar
nutrients
15 g/½ oz citric or malic acid
pectic enzyme
wine yeast

Wash the roots well and slice into 4 litres/6 pints cold water. Boil with the cloves and crushed ginger until the slices are tender. Strain the hot liquid into a bowl or bin containing the crushed Campden tablets, sugar and nutrients. Stir to dissolve. When the liquid is cool add the acid and the pectic enzyme. Cover.

The next day add the yeast, pour into a fermentation vessel, make up to volume with water (5 litres/1 gallon) and keep at 20–25°C/70–75°F. Insert the air-lock when frothing ceases. Continue as directed for a sweet wine on page 45 when gas bubbles no longer form.

Variation

Sustitute 60 ml/2 fl oz orange juice for the citric or malic acid.

· PEA POD WINE ·

(pale fawn, sweet, social wine wine)

2½ kg/5 lb pea pods
water
3 Campden tablets
1⅓ kg/2¾ lb white sugar
nutrients
15 g/½ oz citric or malic acid
pectic enzyme
wine yeast

Wash the pods clean and simmer in 4 litres/6 pints water until tender. Strain the liquid into a bowl or bin containing the crushed Campden tablets, sugar, nutrients and acid, stir well. When cool add the pectic enzyme and cover. The next day add the yeast, pour into a fermentation vessel, make up to volume with water (5 litres/1 gallon) and keep at 20–25°C/70–75°F. Insert the air-lock when frothing ceases. Continue as for a sweet wine on page 45 when gas bubbles no longer form.

Variation

Mangetout can be substituted for pea pods.

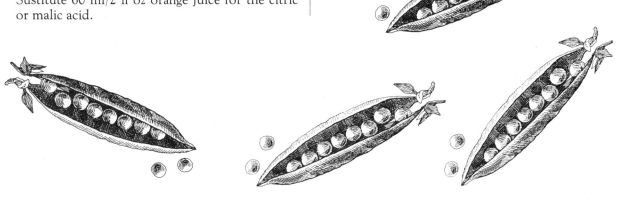

Above: Many vegetables make rather bland wines and need the addition of fresh and dried fruit to produce a good flavour.
Below: Cereal wines are made by mixing the crushed grain with sugar, fresh or dried fruit, or concentrated grape juice.

· POTATO WINE 1 ·

(fawn, sweet, dessert wine)

500 g/1 lb wheat
water
1 kg/2 lb old potatoes
1 kg/2 lb raisins *or* sultanas
2 Campden tablets
1 kg/2 lb demerara sugar
1 orange, rind and juice
1 lemon, rind and juice
nutrients
pectic enzyme
wine yeast

Avoid potatoes with green or black segments or cut out such areas if they are small. Place the wheat in water 24 hours before making the wine.

Scrub the potatoes clean, cut in half and drop into 4 litres/6 pints boiling water. Boil until the segments are just soft, then strain the hot liquid on to the chopped raisins, drained and minced wheat, crushed Campden tablets, sugar, the grated rinds and juices of the orange and lemon and the nutrients. Stir to dissolve the soluble ingredients. When cool, stir in the pectic enzyme and leave covered overnight.

Add the yeast the next day and keep covered at 15–20°C/60–70°F for seven days, stirring twice daily. Strain the liquid into a fermentation vessel, make up to volume with water (5 litres/1 gallon) and continue keeping warm. Insert the air-lock when frothing ceases and finish as for a sweet wine on page 45 when gas bubbles no longer form.

Variation

Substitute pearl barley for wheat.

· POTATO WINE 2 ·

(fawn, sweet, spiced, country wine)

2½ kg/5 lb potatoes
water
2 oranges, rind and juice
2 lemons, rind and juice
15 g/½ oz root ginger
3 Campden tablets
2 kg/4 lb demerara sugar
nutrients
pectic enzyme
wine yeast

Use well-scrubbed, small, old potatoes and bring to the boil in 4 litres/6 pints water. Simmer gently until the potatoes are tender but the skins unbroken. Strain and to the hot liquid add the thinly peeled fruit rinds and the bruised ginger. Boil the liquid for another 15 minutes and then pour it on to the crushed Campden tablets, sugar and nutrients. Stir until dissolved. When cool add the pectic enzyme and fruit juices and leave covered.

The next day add the yeast, keep covered at 15–20°C/60–70°F for three days, strain and pour into the fermentation vessel. Make up to volume with water (5 litres/1 gallon), keep warm, inserting the air-lock when frothing ceases. Continue as directed for a sweet wine on page 45 when no more gas bubbles form.

Above: Juice can be extracted from fruit using a double boiler.
Below: The juice is separated from the pulp by squeezing it through a jelly bag.

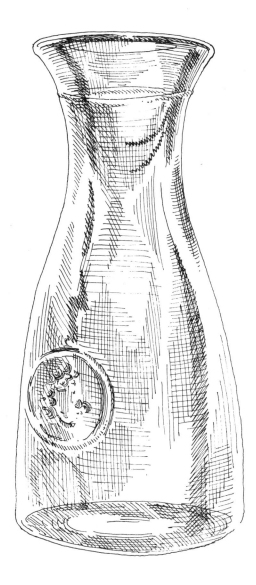

· POTATO WINE 3 ·

(fawn, sweet, country wine)

6 large old potatoes
water
500 g/1 lb green grapes, crushed
500 g/1 lb raisins, chopped
3 Campden tablets
1 kg/2 lb demerara sugar
1 orange, rind and juice
1 lemon, rind and juice
nutrients
pectic enzyme
wine yeast

Avoid potatoes with green or black segments or cut out such areas if they are small. Scrub the potatoes clean, cut in half and drop into 4 litres/6 pints boiling water. Boil until the segments are just soft, then strain the hot liquid on to the grapes, raisins, crushed Campden tablets, sugar, the grated rinds and juices of the orange and lemon and the nutrients. Stir to dissolve the soluble ingredients. When cool stir in the pectic enzyme and leave covered overnight.

Add the yeast the next day and keep covered at 15–20°C/60–70°F for seven days, stirring twice daily. Strain the liquid into a fermentation vessel, make up to volume with water (5 litres/1 gallon) and continue keeping warm. Insert the air-lock when frothing ceases and finish as directed for a sweet wine on page 45 when the gas bubbles no longer form.

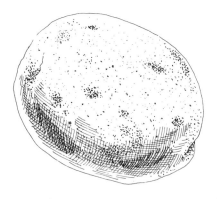

· POTATO WINE 4 ·

(fawn, sweet, country wine)

500 g/1 lb wheat
water
4 large old potatoes
1 kg/2 lb raisins, chopped
3 Campden tablets
1 kg/2 lb demerara sugar
1 orange, rind and juice
1 lemon, rind and juice
nutrients
pectic enzyme
wine yeast

Avoid potatoes with green or black segments or cut out such areas if they are small. Place the wheat in water 24 hours before starting to make the wine.

Scrub the potatoes clean, cut in half and drop into 4 litres/6 pints boiling water. Boil until the segments are just soft, then strain the hot liquid on to the chopped raisins, drained and minced wheat, crushed Campden tablets, sugar, the grated rinds and juices of the orange and lemon and the nutrients. Stir to dissolve the soluble ingredients. When cool stir in the pectic enzyme and leave covered overnight.

Add the yeast the next day and keep covered at 15–20°C/60–70°F for seven days, stirring twice daily. Strain the liquid into a fermentation vessel, make up to volume with water (5 litres/1 gallon) and keep warm. Insert the air-lock when frothing ceases. Continue as directed for a sweet wine on page 45 when the gas bubbles no longer form.

· POTATO WINE 5 ·

(fawn, sweet, country wine)

500 g/1 lb wheat
water
500 g/1 lb large old potatoes
500 g/1 lb prunes, chopped
3 Campden tablets
1 kg/2 lb demerara sugar
1 orange, rind and juice
1 lemon, rind and juice
nutrients
pectic enzyme
wine yeast

Place the wheat in water 24 hours before making the wine. Scrub the potatoes clean, after cutting out any green or black areas. Cut in half and drop into 4 litres/6 pints boiling water. Boil until the segments are just soft, then strain the hot liquid on to the prunes, the drained and minced wheat, crushed Campden tablets, sugar, the grated rinds and juices of the orange and lemon and the nutrients. Stir to dissolve the soluble ingredients. When cool stir in the pectic enzyme and leave covered overnight.

Add the yeast the next day and keep covered at 15–20°C/60–70°F for seven days, stirring twice daily. Strain the liquid into a fermentation vessel, make up to volume with water (5 litres/1 gallon) and keep warm. Insert the air-lock when frothing ceases and finish as directed for a sweet wine on page 45 when the gas bubbles no longer form.

Variations

1. Dried figs can be substituted for prunes.
2. The following can be substituted for potatoes: *eddoes* peel and slice before boiling until soft; *sweet potatoes* wash and peel first; *yams* wash and peel first and add 25 ml/1 fl oz bottled lemon juice to the water in which they are boiled to prevent browning of the tissues.

· RHUBARB WINE 1 ·

(rosé, dry, table wine)

2 kg/4 lb rhubarb stalks
water
2 Campden tablets
pectic enzyme
1 kg/2 lb white sugar
nutrients
wine yeast

Pick the rhubarb stalks in mid-May and discard the leaves. Wipe the stalks clean, slice thinly into 4 litres/6 pints cold water in which the Campden tablets have been dissolved and the pectic enzyme stirred in. Leave covered for two days, stirring at intervals, then strain but do *not* squeeze the residue.

Dissolve the sugar and nutrients in the liquid, add the yeast, pour into a fermentation vessel and make up to volume with water (5 litres/1 gallon). Keep at 15–20°C/60–70°F, inserting the air-lock when frothing ceases and continue as for a dry wine on page 44 when gas bubbles no longer form.

Rhubarb wine may not ferment entirely to dryness, even with the addition of nutrients. If this happens, keep the syphoned wine in the filled storage jar under a storage bung for several months.

This is a very good wine in its own right and also makes an excellent base for a sparkling wine (page 48), or for being flavoured with low acid fruits, flowers and herbs (Blackberry Wine 3, page 70)

Variation

Young red stalks of the Champagne rhubarb give a deeper coloured, rosé wine.

· RHUBARB WINE 2 ·

(light fawn, sweet, social wine)

2½ kg/5 lb rhubarb stalks
water
2 Campden tablets
pectic enzyme
2 lemons, juice
1¾ kg/3½ lb demerara or white sugar
nutrients
wine yeast

Cut off and discard the leaves. Clean and dry the stalks, cut into short sections and crush. Put in a bowl or bin, pour on 4 litres/6 pints cold water, dissolve the Campden tablets in the liquid and add the pectic enzyme and lemon juice. Leave covered for three days, stirring twice daily.

Strain off the pulp and run the liquid into a fermentation vessel to which the sugar and nutrients have been added. Shake to dissolve. Add the yeast and make up to volume with water (5 litres/ 1 gallon). Keep at 15–20°C/60–70°F, inserting the air-lock when frothing ceases.

Continue as directed for a sweet wine on page 45 when the gas bubbles no longer form.

· RHUBARB WINE 3 ·

(fawn, sweet, country wine)

250 g/½ lb raisins *or* sultanas
2½ kg/5 lb rhubarb stalks
3 Campden tablets
pectic enzyme
nutrients
water
2 kg/4 lb white sugar
wine yeast
6 egg shells

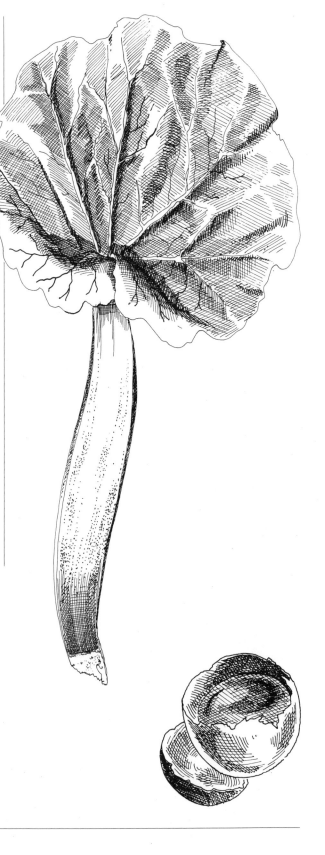

Add the chopped raisins to the sliced, clean rhubarb stalks (no green leaves), crushed Campden tablets, pectic enzyme, nutrients and 4 litres/6 pints cold water in a bowl or bin. Stir well. Dissolve in the sugar and add the yeast the next day. Leave covered at 15–20°C/60–70°F for five days. Stir and crush with a wooden spoon twice a day.

Strain and run the liquid into a fermentation vessel containing the crushed egg shells (or 15 g/½ oz precipitated chalk instead). Make up to volume with water (5 litres/1 gallon), continue to keep warm, inserting the air-lock when frothing ceases. Finish as directed for a sweet wine on page 45 when the gas bubbles no longer form.

Variations

Substitute 245 g/8½ oz concentrated white grape juice for the raisins/sultanas.

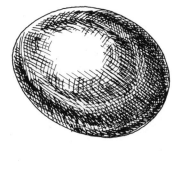

· RHUBARB & · BLACKBERRY PORT

(red, sweet, country wine)

rhubarb wine, dry
1½ kg/3 lb blackberries
water

In May, prepare rhubarb wine as directed in the recipe for Rhubarb Wine 1 and hold the fermented dry wine in the filled and sealed storage jar after its first syphoning (page 132). Cover the ripe blackberries with 600 ml/1 pint water and bring to the boil. Simmer for a few minutes and pour through a cloth or nylon straining bag. Then strain again through several layers of muslin or a jelly bag. Add to the rhubarb wine and keep cool in a filled jar, sealed with a storage bung, for four months.

If the wine ferments treat as directed for a sweet wine on page 45 as though the first batch of sugar had been added to the stored wine.

· SPINACH WINE ·

(fawn, sweet, country wine)

1 kg/2 lb spinach
water
500 g/1 lb raisins *or* sultanas
2 Campden tablets
1½ kg/3 lb white sugar
nutrients
pectic enzyme
1 orange, juice
1 lemon, juice
wine yeast

Wash and drain the spinach and boil in 4 litres/6 pints water for 30 minutes. Strain the liquid on to the chopped raisins, crushed Campden tablets, sugar and nutrients. When cool, add the pectic enzyme and fruit juices and leave covered.

Add the yeast the next day and keep covered at 15–20°C/60–70°F for seven days, stirring twice daily. Strain the liquid into a fermentation vessel, make up to volume with water (5 litres/1 gallon) and keep warm. Insert the air-lock when frothing ceases. Finish as directed for a sweet wine on page 45 when the gas bubbles no longer form.

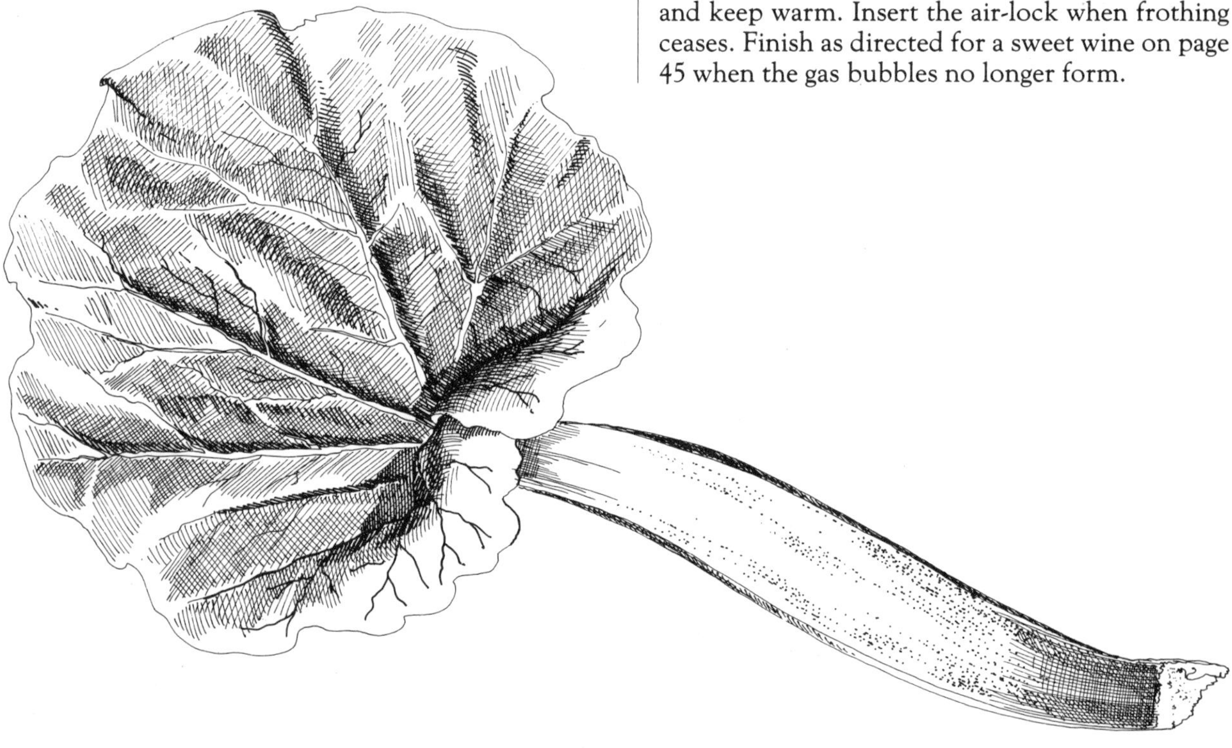

CEREAL WINES

Cereals contain very little fermentable sugar but a great deal of starch. With one or two rare exceptions, yeasts cannot ferment starch so the grains act mainly as a source of yeast food and wine flavouring. The starch can be broken down if the grain is malted (i.e. allowed to germinate and then dried after removal of sprouts and roots).

Traditionally, cereal wines are made by mixing the crushed grain or malt extract with sugar, fresh or dried fruit (raisins, sultanas etc.) or concentrated grape juice. The grains can be crushed easily if first soaked overnight in about 1¼ litres/2 pints water. Otherwise use flaked or kibbled grain. Thereafter the chopped/crushed ingredients are treated with boiling water. When cool the extract is yeasted to utilise the solubilised sugars and to produce alcohol, flavour etc. There are a number of commercial kits for making cereal based wines, e.g. rice and raisin.

· BARLEY WINE 1 ·

(fawn, sweet, country wine)

500 g/1 lb old potatoes
3 Campden tablets
1¼ kg/2½ lb white or demerara sugar
500 g/1 lb barley (chicken or pearl)
500 g/1 lb raisins *or* sultanas, chopped
2 lemons
water
wine yeast

Scrub the potatoes, cut up small (after removing any green or black sections) and put the pieces in a bowl or bin, followed by the crushed Campden tablets, sugar, crushed barley, chopped raisins and thinly sliced lemons. Add 4 litres/6 pints boiling water and stir until the tablets and sugar have dissolved.

Add the yeast the next day and keep covered at 15–20°C/60–70°F. When frothing ceases, strain and pour the liquid into a fermentation vessel. Make up to volume with water (5 litres/1 gallon), insert the air-lock and continue keeping warm until gas bubbles cease to form. Finish as directed for a sweet wine on page 45.

Variations

1. Use 1½ kg/3 lb crushed barley, 1 kg/2 lb raisins and 1 kg/2 lb white sugar and follow the recipe above.
2. Ferment the mixture in a covered bowl or bin, having made up to volume (5 litres/1 gallon), instead of 'until frothing ceases', then strain. This gives a more intense flavour.

· BARLEY WINE 2 ·

(fawn, sweet, social wine)

3 Campden tablets
1½ kg/3 lb white sugar
500 g/1 lb barley
245 g/8½ oz concentrated white grape juice
10 g/⅓ oz citric acid
water
wine yeast

Place in a bowl or bin the crushed Campden tablets, sugar, crushed barley, grape concentrate and citric acid. Add 4 litres/6 pints boiling water and stir until the soluble ingredients have dissolved. Add the yeast next day and keep covered at 15–20°C/60–70°F. When frothing ceases, strain and pour the liquid into a fermentation vessel. Make up to volume with water (5 litres/1 gallon), insert the air-lock and continue keeping warm until the gas bubbles cease to form.

Finish as directed for a sweet wine on page 45.

Variation

Pure orange juice (60 ml/2 fl oz) may be substituted for the citric acid. If the stored wine does not clear, treat with pectic enzyme.

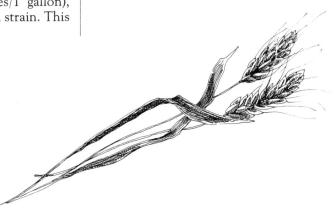

· BARLEY WINE 3 ·

(deep fawn, sweet, social wine)

1 kg/2 lb barley
3 Campden tablets
1 kg/2 lb white sugar
500 g/1 lb malt extract
500 g/1 lb raisins, chopped
water
90 ml/3 fl oz pure orange juice
wine yeast
starch enzyme

Place the crushed barley, crushed Campden tablets, sugar, malt extract and raisins in a bowl or bin. Add 4 litres/6 pints boiling water and stir until the soluble ingredients have dissolved. Add the orange juice when cool.

Add the yeast and starch enzyme the next day. Keep covered at 15–20°C/60–70°F for three weeks, stirring occasionally. Strain and pour the liquid into a fermentation vessel. Make up to volume with water if necessary (5 litres/1 gallon). Insert the air-lock and continue keeping warm until gas bubbles cease to form.

Finish as directed for a sweet wine on page 45. If the stored wine does not clear, treat with pectic enzyme.

· MAIZE WINE ·

(fawn, sweet, country wine)

4 oranges, rind and juice
1 lemon, rind and juice
500 g/1 lb raisins, chopped
2 Campden tablets
2¼ kg/4½ lb demerara sugar
750 g/1½ lb crushed maize
water
wine yeast

Thinly peel the oranges and lemon and drop the rind into a bowl or bin with the raisins, crushed Campden tablets, sugar, maize and fruit juices. Pour on 4 litres/6 pints boiling water.

Add the yeast the next day and keep covered at 15–20°C/60–70°F. When the frothing ceases, strain and pour the liquid into a fermentation vessel. Make up to volume with water (5 litres/1 gallon), insert the air-lock and continue keeping warm until the gas bubbles cease to form.

Finish as directed for a sweet wine on page 45.

· MALT WINE ·

(fawn, sweet, country wine)

1 kg/2 lb malt extract
3 Campden tablets
500 g/1 lb white sugar
500 g/1 lb white honey
15 g/$\frac{1}{2}$ oz citric acid
water
wine yeast

Place the malt extract in a bowl or bin, followed by the crushed Campden tablets, sugar, honey and citric acid. Add 4 litres/6 pints boiling water and stir until the tablets and sugar have dissolved.

Add the yeast next day and keep covered at 15–20°C/60–70°F. When frothing ceases, strain and pour the liquid into a fermentation vessel. Make up to volume with water (5 litres/1 gallon), insert the air-lock and continue keeping warm until gas bubbles cease to form.

Finish as directed for a sweet wine on page 45.

· RICE WINE ·

(fawn, sweet, social wine)

1$\frac{1}{2}$ kg/3 lb patna or any long grain rice
2 Campden tablets
1 kg/2 lb white sugar
15 g/$\frac{1}{2}$ oz citric acid
500 g/1 lb raisins, chopped
water
wine yeast

Wash the rice in a sieve under cold running water. Crush the rice and add to the crushed Campden tablets, sugar, citric acid and raisins in a bowl or bin. Add 4 litres/6 pints boiling water. Stir until the soluble ingredients have dissolved.

Add the yeast next day and keep covered at 15–20°C/60–70°F for 12 days, stirring occasionally. When frothing ceases, strain and pour the liquid into a fermentation vessel. Make up to volume with water (5 litres/1 gallon), insert the air-lock and continue keeping warm until gas bubbles cease to form.

Finish as directed for a sweet wine on page 45.

This is not the Japanese rice wine, known as Saké, for which a special mould and yeast and a complex brewing procedure are required.

Variation

Do not crush the washed rice or chop up the raisins. Use the other ingredients but increase the amount of boiling water to 5 litres/1 gallon. Ferment to dryness in the covered bowl or bin, before straining the liquid. Continue as directed for a sweet wine on page 45.

· WHEAT WINE ·

(fawn, sweet, social wine)

500 g/1 lb wheat
water
2 Campden tablets
1 kg/2 lb demerara sugar
1 kg/2 lb raisins
3 oranges
1 lemon
wine yeast

Soak the wheat overnight in 1$\frac{1}{4}$ litres/2 pints water. The next day, drain and crush the wheat and drop it into a bowl or bin, followed by the crushed Campden tablets, sugar, chopped raisins and thinly sliced oranges and lemon. Add 4 litres/6 pints boiling water and stir until the tablets and sugar have dissolved.

Add the yeast next day and keep covered at 15–20°C/60–70°F. When frothing ceases, strain and pour the liquid into a fermentation vessel. Make up to volume with water (5 litres/1 gallon), insert the air-lock and continue keeping warm until gas bubbles cease to form.

Finish as directed for a sweet wine on page 45.

FRUIT JUICES,
CORDIALS & SYRUPS

*F*ruit juices, cordials and syrups should not contain any alcohol. The yeasts and bacteria naturally present in the raw material must be killed or their growth prevented, otherwise the juices and syrups will ferment in bottle, which would then explode violently. The cordials are made and served hot so the problem does not arise. The heat sterilised products must also be kept refrigerated once opened because they contain no preservative. They then have a limited shelf life, being susceptible eventually to the growth of airborne mould spores.

It needs a considerable amount of fruit to prepare these products so it is economical to make juices, cordials, and syrups from fruits surplus to normal requirements and that otherwise would be wasted, or to use fruit available from the hedgerow. Some of the exotic fruits make interesting variations on the more usual flavours. Descriptions of these fruits are given in Exotic Wines (page 90). Vegetables and low acid fruits (e.g. tomatoes, melons, figs) should not be made into non-alcoholic products without adding acid (citric or malic). Their natural

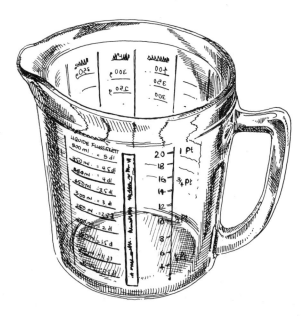

low acidity makes ordinary methods of heat sterilisation ineffective and spores of food poisoning bacteria could develop.

Instead of heat sterilising juices and syrups, they can be deep frozen in suitably stoppered beverage containers, allowing space for the expansion due to ice formation. Once thawed, the juice or syrup should be refrigerated and used up within one week or less.

Juices and nectars are valuable for preserving the nutritional properties of fruits, and are thus especially valuable for children. Juices can always be drunk as such, while syrups can be diluted with iced – or sparkling water in summer and with hot water in winter. Milk can be flavoured with syrups, but care is needed to prevent it from curdling, so keep the cold milk stirred briskly, while slowly adding the syrup. Usually one part of syrup is added to five or six parts of milk. Fruit juices can also be used in puddings, jellies, ice creams and sorbets or poured over the last two to give extra flavour and nourishment.

Methods of extracting juice, for juices and syrups are described in Juice Extraction and Treatment (pages 27–31) and, with the exception of pulp fermentation, can be used equally well here. Two methods of syrup making are described in detail below. Fruits for juice, cordials and syrup making should be well ripened, free of moulds and washed clean. Remove any leaves or largish stems.

◆ Hot Method

1. Place the fruit in a basin or a double saucepan and bruise well with a wooden spoon, pulper or masher. Add about 60 ml/2 fl oz of water (more for blackcurrants) and stand in a saucepan half-filled with water. Cover and simmer gently until the juice flows freely, if necessary refilling the outer saucepan with more water to prevent it boiling dry. Once the juice is flowing freely, repulp.

Alternatively, the fruit may be heated with a little water in a saucepan and heated directly. Keep stirring the fruit to prevent sticking and mash with a wooden spoon. Once the mixture has come to the boil, keep it on the heat for only a few more minutes.

Another alternative is to put the roughly chopped fruit in a steam extractor, heat the water reservoir and collect the juice issuing from the outlet spout.

2. Squeeze the pulp in a jelly bag, a thick cloth or a nylon straining

bag. To each 600 ml/1 pint juice add 375–500 g/¾–1 lb white sugar. Stir until the sugar dissolves and, if necessary, restrain or filter with a filter aid.

3. The syrup must be bottled as soon as possible and sterilised to kill any yeasts present. Fill small bottles leaving 4–5 cm/1½–2 in. below the base of the cork, screw stopper or crown cork. If corks are used, wire or tie them down strongly or else they may be forced out during heating. The corks or stoppers must be sterilised by submerging them in boiling water for 15 minutes before use. Put the stoppered bottles in a deep pan fitted with a false bottom (i.e. a fish kettle) and pour in sufficient water to come to the bases of the corks or stoppers. Heat the water to simmering and maintain for 20 minutes. Take the bottles out and stand them on a plain wooden table or breadboard to cool.

◆ Cold Method

Syrups made by this method are fresher in flavour than hot processed syrups but they are slightly more difficult to prepare.

4. Crush the weighed cleaned fruit in a bowl and mix in the amount of pectic enzyme recommended on the packet. Note the recommended temperature since some work more effectively at 40°C/105°F. Leave overnight.

Blackcurrants need longer but not if a second enzyme, Rohament P, is also used.

When the juice from the enzymed pulp gives a negative pectin test (page 151), squeeze the pulp through a thick cloth or nylon straining bag, sweeten the juice, bottle, seal and sterilise as described in 2 and 3 of the Hot Method above.

Some fruits also need the addition of citric acid as the syrups can be a little insipid. Where necessary it will be specified in the recipe. All syrups should be kept in the dark and as cold as convenient to retain colour and flavour. Most syrups tend to throw a sediment of particles too fine to be retained in the straining cloths. The material forming the deposit is perfectly wholesome but, if a clear product is required, the syrup can be decanted carefully from the bottle when used (the sediment can be added to an appropriate wine fermentation). No syrup should be kept for more than a year as flavour slowly deteriorates.

· CLOUDY APPLE ·
JUICE

2 kg/4 lb Bramley's seedling apples (mature)
6 kg/12 lb dessert apples
2 g ascorbic acid

Mix the apples, mill and press out the juice (page 27). Add the ascorbic acid immediately after pressing to preserve the natural opalescence and to counter oxidation. Strain the juice through organdie, fine nylon or several layers of muslin. Bottle, seal and sterilise as described in paragraph **3** (page 141).

Depending on the apple varieties and their maturity, the appearance of the cloudy juice may range from a faint pearliness to a marked turbidity, with a varying amount of deposit formed by apple solids. Before serving, the bottle should be chilled, then shaken before pouring to preserve the maximum apple flavour.

· CLEAR APPLE ·
JUICE

2 g ascorbic acid
8 kg/16 lb apples
pectic enzyme
Bentonite

Add half the ascorbic acid to the freshly pressed juice (page 27). Treat with pectic enzyme as described in paragraph **4** (page 141). Fine the juice with Bentonite (page 26) to prevent a protein haze forming when the juice is later chilled before drinking.

After fining syphon off the clear juice, leaving the deposit behind. Filter, if possible, and add the remaining ascorbic acid. Bottle, seal and sterilise as described in paragraph **3** (page 141).

· APPLE & ORANGE ·
JUICE BLEND

white sugar
4 litres/6 pints cloudy apple juice
600 ml/1 pint pure orange juice
2 g ascorbic acid

Make up a sugar syrup by boiling 500 g/1 lb white sugar in 1 litre/33 fl oz water. Mix the ingredients, bottle, seal and sterilise as described in paragraph **3** (page 141).

Variations

1. Cloudy and clear apple juice can be flavoured with *blackcurrant*, *strawberry* and other syrups according to taste.

2. See page 90 for suggestions on the use of *tropical fruits* substituting apple juice for white wine. Always sterilise the bottled mixtures as described in paragraph **3** (page 141) unless the syrups are frozen or drunk immediately after making.

· APRICOT SYRUP ·

1½ kg/3 lb white sugar

4 litres/6 pints water

3 kg/6 lb apricots

Boil the sugar and water together to make a syrup. Drop in the halved and stoned apricots and simmer until they are tender, replacing any water that has boiled away. Remove the apricots and, if wished, add a sprig of flowering clary and simmer for a few minutes more. Strain, bottle, seal and sterilise as described in paragraph **3** (page 141).

Variation

Substitute *peaches* for apricots in the above recipe.

· BLACKBERRY · SYRUP

3 kg/6 lb blackberries

300 ml/½ pint water

white sugar

Stew the berries very gently in the inner compartment of a double saucepan with the water for an hour. Squeeze out the juice, add 500 g/1 lb sugar to each 600 ml/1 pint of juice and simmer for 10 minutes. Allow to cool, bottle seal and sterilise as described in paragraph **3** (page 141).

Variation

Add 15 g/½ oz whole cloves in a muslin bag during the second simmering and remove before bottling.

· BLACK CHERRY · SYRUP

3 kg/6 lb black cherries

300 ml/½ pint water

500 g/1 lb white sugar (per 600 ml/1 pint juice)

pectic enzyme (cold method)

Prepare by the hot or cold processing methods from de-stoned fruit following the details given in paragraphs **1** to **4** (pages 140–141).

· BLACKCURRANT · SYRUP

1½ kg/3 lb blackcurrants

600 ml/1 pint water

white sugar

Stew the berries very gently in a double saucepan with the water for an hour. Squeeze out the juice, add 500 g/1 lb white sugar to each 600 ml/1 pint of juice and simmer for 10 minutes. Allow to cool, bottle seal and sterilise as described in paragraph **3** (page 141).

· DAMSON SYRUP ·

3 kg/6 lb damsons

300 ml/½ pint water

500 g/1 lb white sugar (per 600 ml/1 pint juice)

pectic enzyme (cold method)

Prepare by the hot or cold processing methods given in paragraphs **1** to **4** (see pages 140–141).

· ELDERBERRY ·
SYRUP

3 kg/6 lb elderberries
300 ml/½ pint water
500 g/1 lb white sugar (per 600 ml/1 pint juice)
pectic enzyme (cold method)

Prepare by the hot or cold processing methods given in paragraphs **1** to **4** (see pages 140–141).

Variation

Add six cloves and a small piece of bruised ginger or 8 g/¼ oz each of allspice, cinnamon stick and mace, to each 1¼ litres/2 pints unsweetened juice and simmer for 10 to 15 minutes. Strain before sweetening, bottling, sealing and sterilising.

· ELDERFLOWER ·
SYRUP

1¼ litres/2 pints elderflowers
water
white sugar
lemon juice

Collect elderflowers in full blossom on a dry day and shake the florets into a preserving pan. Just cover with water, simmer for 30 minutes, replacing any water that boils away. Strain and squeeze out the liquid and return it to the pan. Add 500 g/ 1 lb white sugar and the juice of a lemon to each 600 ml/1 pint liquid and simmer again for 10 minutes, skimming if necessary. Allow to cool, bottle, seal and sterilise as directed in paragraph **3** (page 141). The syrup can either be used as a base for a cooling summer drink or for making water ices.

· GINGER & LEMON ·
SYRUP

90 g/3 oz root ginger
1 lemon, rind and juice
1¼ litres/2 pints water
white sugar

Bruise the ginger and put into a saucepan with the water and the thinly sliced lemon rind. Bring to the boil and simmer gently for 45 minutes replenishing any water that boils away.

Strain and to every 600 ml/1 pint of liquid add 500 g/1 lb sugar and the strained lemon juice. Bottle, seal and sterilise as directed in paragraph **3** (page 141).

Put 25 ml/1 fl oz of syrup in a tumbler and fill with hot or iced water as required. Decorate with a slice of lemon.

· GRAPE JUICE ·

8 kg/16 lb grapes
1 Campden tablet
2 g ascorbic acid

White juice is made from white grapes, using either the hot or cold method, or white fleshed, red skinned grapes using direct pressing or the cold method. Red and black grapes give a red juice with the hot method.

Extract the juice from the grapes. As the juice darkens readily after pressing add one Campden tablet per 5 litres/1 gallon, as well as the ascorbic acid. Strain the juice through organdie, fine nylon or several layers of muslin. Bottle, seal and sterilise as described in paragraph **3** (page 141). Crystals of cream of tartar may form on standing. The juice can be decanted easily from the deposit when the bottle is opened and served.

Grape juice can be blended with the juices of other fruits. In unfavourable seasons, poorly ripened cold house or outdoor grapes can be converted into juice with the addition of sugar, or sugar syrup to dilute the high acidity.

Grape juice is a very refreshing summer drink.

· GRAPE SYRUP ·

8 kg/16 lb grapes (well coloured)
water
white sugar

Wash the grapes, drain, remove the stalks and place in a saucepan. Just cover with water and simmer until the juice is well extracted. Stir during heating and replace any water that boils away.

Pour into a jelly bag and leave to drip overnight. Do not squeeze or the juice will become cloudy. To each 1¼ litres/2 pints juice add 500 g/ 1 lb sugar, return to the heat and simmer, stirring until the sugar is dissolved. Strain, bottle, seal and sterilise as directed in paragraph **3** (page 141).

Quarter fill a tumbler with the syrup and dilute with water.

· LEMON SYRUP ·

2 kg/4 lb white sugar
1¼ litres/2 pints water
6 lemons (large), juice and rind

Dissolve the sugar in the slightly warmed water and add the lemon juice and finely grated rind. Stir vigorously, leave covered for 12 hours, strain, bottle, seal and sterilise as described in paragraph **3** (page 141).

· LEMON & ORANGE · SYRUP

3 kg/6 lb white sugar
2½ litres/4 pints water
lemons, rind and juice
oranges, rind and juice
15 g/½ oz citric acid

Prepare a syrup from the sugar and water and boil gently for five minutes with the thinly peeled rinds of one lemon and one orange.

Squeeze the juice from an equal number of lemons and oranges until there is the same volume of juice as syrup. Mix the two liquids together, dissolve the citric acid in it. Strain, bottle, seal and sterilise as directed in paragraph **3** (page 141).

· LOGANBERRY · SYRUP

3 kg/6 lb loganberries
pectic enzyme (cold method)
300 ml/½ pint water
white sugar

Prepare by the hot or cold processing method given in paragraphs **1** to **4** (pages 140–141) dissolving 500 g/1 lb white sugar in every 600 ml/1 pint of juice.

Variation

Substitute *mulberries* or *raspberries* or *strawberries* for loganberries in the recipe above.

Above: A selection of home-made fruit juices.
Below: Juices can be produced from a wide variety of fruits.

· NETTLE SYRUP ·

1 kg/2 lb young nettle tops
2½ litres/4 pints water
white sugar

Wash and drain the nettle tops. Simmer gently with the water for an hour, replacing any water that has boiled away. Strain and dissolve 500 g/ 1 lb sugar in each 600 ml/1 pint of liquid. Bottle, seal and sterilise as directed in paragraph **3** (page 141).

According to old country wisdom, the syrup was said to be valuable as a blood purifier. It is also used with iced soda to make a cooling drink.

· ORANGE SYRUP ·

2 kg/4 lb white sugar
2 litres/3 pints water
6 oranges, rind and juice
15 g/½ oz citric acid

Gentle boil the sugar, water and thinly peeled orange rinds together for 10 minutes. Leave covered overnight and then add the acid and orange juice. Strain, bottle, seal and sterilise as directed in paragraph **3** (page 141).

· RHUBARB ·
CORDIAL

1 kg/2 lb rhubarb
120 g/4 oz white sugar
1¼ litres/2 pints water
2 cloves
8 g/¼ oz root ginger
mint leaves

Cut off and discard the rhubarb leaves. In winter, use young stems of forced rhubarb or canned rhubarb in syrup. In the latter case there is no need to add sugar, measure the volume of syrup and make up to 1¼ litres/2 pints with water.

Gently simmer the chopped rhubarb stalks, sugar, water (or syrup), cloves and bruised ginger in a saucepan until the rhubarb is soft. If using canned rhubarb, simmer for 10 minutes. Strain and serve in warmed glasses decorated with a few mint leaves.

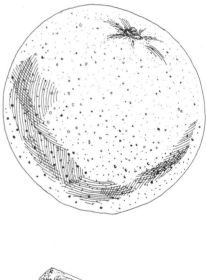

· ROSEHIP SYRUP ·

1 kg/2 lb ripe rosehips
2¾ litres/4½ pints water
500 g/1 lb white sugar

Mince the cleaned rosehips and drop immediately into a saucepan containing 2 litres/3 pints boiling water. Bring to the boil straight away, then remove the saucepan from the heat and leave for 15 minutes. Pour through a scalded jelly bag and allow to drip.

Return the pulp to the saucepan, add the remaining 900 ml/1½ pints water, re-boil and allow to stand without further boiling for another 10 minutes. Drain through the jelly bag as before. Combine the two extracts in a saucepan and simmer until the volume is reduced to 900 ml/1½ pints. Add the sugar and re-boil for a further five minutes. Bottle (use small ones), seal and sterilise as directed in paragraph **3** (page 141).

The flavour can be varied by mixing with orange or lemon syrups and diluting with soda or sparkling spa water.

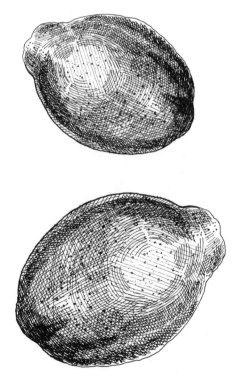

· ROSE SYRUP ·

500 g/1 lb rhubarb
600 ml/1 pint water
500 g/1 lb white sugar
10 red roses, petals

Cut the rhubarb in mid-May, remove the leaves, clean the stalks and cut into chunks. Simmer in the water for 20 minutes, mashing with a wooden spoon to assist the extraction of juice.

Strain, add the sugar and detached rose petals to the liquid and simmer for 15 minutes. Strain and gently boil the liquid until it thickens. Pour into heated bottles, seal and sterilise as directed in paragraph **3** (page 141).

To use, put 5 ml/1 tsp syrup in a glass and add 30 ml/1 tbsp boiling water. When cold, fill with milk. It was once said to be a good cure for sore throat and an excellent pick-me-up.

· WINTER CORDIAL ·

60 g/2 oz fine oatmeal
30 g/1 oz demerara sugar
1 lemon, rind and juice
15 g/½ oz ground ginger
1 litre/2 pints water

Mix the oatmeal, sugar, thinly peeled lemon rind and ground ginger in a saucepan. Pour in the lemon juice and boiling water and stir until the sugar dissolves. Simmer the mixture for 10 minutes, strain and serve hot.

PROBLEMS OF WINE-MAKING

With the correct choice of juice treatment, yeast strain, fermentation and storage treatments, there should be no problems in making your own wines (or juices, cordials and syrups). Problems may occur due to seasonal variations in the composition of the raw material, or because standards of hygiene have been neglected.

The following catalogue of horrors may sound a little unnerving to the hopeful wine-maker, but it should be considered in the same light as a book on first aid. Provided the methods given in the recipes are adhered to, there should be no need for wine or syrup to undergo any of these disorders. Problems that can occur are: faulty or 'stuck' fermentation; hazes and deposits; colour changes; peculiar aromas and flavours.

Methods for treating such problems are outlined below (see also Specialised Wine-Making Ingredients pages 24–26).

· 'STUCK' FERMENTATION ·

Fermentation can cease prematurely for several reasons. The liquid may contain non-fermentable solids, the osmotic pressure may be wrong, or the nutrient supply inadequate. The yeast strain may be unsuitable or the fermenting temperature incorrect or there could be competing microflora.

Cases where unwanted fermentations can occur are also discussed.

Non-fermentable solids. Some raw materials contain sufficient non-sugar solids to give a positive reading on the hydrometer, yet contain no sugars fermentable by normal fermenting yeasts (e.g. sorbitol in pears). Check with the diabetic sugar test (Clinitest) on page 50.

Osmotic pressure. A combination of high sugar and alcohol content will stop the growth of most fermenting yeasts. When making a high alcohol or a stable sweet wine, it is better to add the sugar in portions at intervals during the fermentation. (It should cause no trouble when making dry table wines of lower alcohol content.)

If wines cease fermenting prematurely, treat with yeast nutrients (page 24) and allow fermentation to go to completion. The recipes in this book are designed to avoid any premature cessation of fermentation due to incorrect sugar/alcohol combinations.

Nutrient supply. Ensure that any concentrated juices used for wine-making have not become dark brown through age or high temperature storage. Such concentrates are difficult to ferment when diluted since they contain fermentation inhibitiors and a deficiency of particular yeast nutrients. Corrective treatment in the home is impracticable.

The recipes specify the addition of yeast nutrients when particular raw materials have an inadequate supply of natural nutrients needed for wine-making. Extracts of flowers and herbs in particular need the addition of yeast nutrients.

Yeast Strain. The yeast used in wine-making is important since different strains vary in their ability to withstand alcohol, to settle out (flocculate) at the end of the fermentation, nutrient requirements etc. A general purpose yeast is suitable for most dry wines, but specialised yeasts should be used for wines such as Sauternes, sherry or high alcohol wines. Use the amount specified on the package and activate as directed. See also Yeast Cultures and Fermentation (page 32). Aeration of the yeast suspension by vigorous shaking for a few minutes before adding ensures a prompt start to fermentation.

Very occasionally a wine will cease fermentation prematurely for no obvious reason and does not respond to the addition of more yeast or nutrients. Aeration with a clean fish tank aerator for 24–48 hours will re-activate yeast growth and fermentation.

Abnormally flocculent yeasts that settle out completely soon after the start of fermentation can also cause normal wine fermentations to cease prematurely. They are, however, useful for making low alcohol wines.

Fermentation temperature. The temperature of fermentation is very important, hence the value of thermostatically controlled heaters (page 13). Too low a temperature, or one that fluctuates widely, will depress the rate of fermentation. The optimum temperature lies between 15–20°C/60–70°F for white wines and 20–25°C/70–75°F for red wines. Lower temperatures merely reduce the rate of fermentation or cause it to cease. Higher temperatures lead to uncontrolled rapid rates of fermentation and killing of the yeast.

The alcohol tolerance of a yeast and its production of flavour components are also related to the fermentation temperature.

Competing microflora. If insufficient acid and sulphur dioxide are added to the extract, it will probably allow the growth of any acetic (vinegar) and/or lactic acid bacteria present in the raw material. Excessive numbers of such bacteria cause premature death of the yeast cells. The problem is aggravated if non- or inadequately sulphited juices are fermented in vessels with pervious or inadequately cleaned surfaces.

Fermentation during storage. Apart from unwanted cessation of fermentation, there are also unwanted fermentations. Explosions in sealed storage jars or bottles can only occur with inadequately stabilised sweet wines. Malo-lactic fermentation in dry wines (page 41) does not produce sufficient gas to cause problems.

It is possible to take no particular precautions and to protect jars or bottles with safety bungs (page 13). Recipes for sweet wines include a technique for making them stable against yeast growth in bottle. As explained in Wine Treatment (page 38), some degree of protection can be given to sweet wines by adding 1 Campden tablet and 1 g sorbic acid per 5 litres/1 gallon just before bottling. These are the usual ingredients of commercial 'wine stabilisers'.

• Summary on faulty fermentations

The recipe describes
• addition of yeast nutrients where necessary
• a juice treatment that prevents the active growth of spoilage bacteria.
Always use
• a suitable strain and quantity of fermenting yeast
• correct fermentation temperature
If fermentation ceases *prematurely*, check that
• too much sugar has not been added
• the fermentation temperature is correct and has not fluctuated widely
• add more nutrients. If this fails, try in turn a fresh yeast culture and aeration until fermentation restarts.

• Fermentation for making high alcohol wines

• use a special alcohol tolerant yeast strain
• incremental feeding of sugars
• add a second dose of yeast nutrients part way through fermentation.

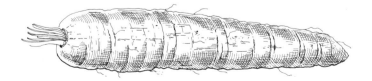

• HAZES & DEPOSITS •

A stored or bottled wine is unsightly if it is not clear or has a deposit. When a jar of fermented wine is transferred to cool storage, clarification should soon start from the surface of the wine. Clearing continues as the yeast settles out to form a deposit. After racking or syphoning off at the stated intervals, the wine should be clear enough to bottle (see also page 41).

Hazes that do not clear naturally can be chemical or microbiological in origin and most of them are preventable.

• Chemical Hazes

Pectin. Gel-forming compounds (polysaccharides) derived originally from raw materials that contained insufficient natural pectin-destroying enzymes, or where the juice was extracted by boiling. Boiling extracts large amounts of soluble pectin and, at the same time, destroys an enzyme which, with another from the fermenting yeast, would normally break down the pectin to simple components during fermentation.

The presence of soluble pectin can be detected by adding 4 tsp methylated spirits to 1 tsp cloudy wine in a glass. A positive result is shown by the formation of a jelly-like clot or strings. The main bulk of hazy wine should be treated with a commercial pectic enzyme (page 25) as directed on the package. Sometimes complete clarity is not achieved, in which case filter afterwards using a filter aid.

Starch. Young root vegetables, potatoes, bananas and cereals contain another polysaccharide, starch, which again is extracted and solubilised by excessive boiling. The slightly viscous wine then stops the yeast from settling out.

Test for starch by treating a few millilitres of wine with tincture of iodine on a white tile. A blue colour indicates starch, in which case treat the main bulk of wine with a starch splitting enzyme (page 25).

Protein. Again the wine does not clarify rapidly and filters only slowly. It is often observed in wines made from commercial concentrated juices, but not those made from concentrates specially prepared for home wine-makers. If a small sample of the wine is filtered and becomes hazy after being chilled for a few days in a refrigerator, a chill

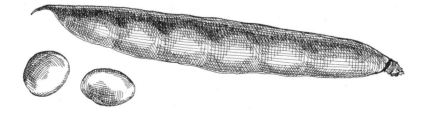

haze due to protein is indicated. Comparison with a similar sample held at room temperature (which does not haze) is helpful.

Alternatively, add a few drops of a 5 per cent tannic acid solution (5 g dissolved in 100 ml distilled water) to 25 ml/1 fl oz wine. If a loose deposit is formed, treat the main bulk of wine with 2–3 g tannic acid, previously dissolved in a little water, or 40–60 ml (1½–2¼ fl oz) of solution, per 5 litres/1 gallon.

The wine can also be treated with Bentonite, prepared previously as a slurry (page 26): 25 ml/1 fl oz per 5 litres/1 gallon is an average dose, more can be added if necessary. Alternatively, protein-destroying enzymes are now available commercially (page 25).

Spiced wines. A haze due to using an excessive amount of spice, leaving the spice too long in contact with the wine or to the use of powdered spices. The haze does not react to the pectin or starch tests, does not have a silky sheen when the contents of the jar are swirled (see lactic acid bacteria, page 153) and does not filter easily. There is just a pale opalescence.

The haze may be removed by fining, try chitin first (page 26). Next time use less spice and never the powdered form unless stated in the recipe.

Excessive oxidation. Wine will develop a haze if left exposed to air at any stage of wine-making in the *absence* of fermentation yeast. It is accentuated if more copper and iron are present than found naturally in the raw material (i.e. derived from unsuitable equipment).

Commercially the wine can be treated but it is then only suitable for blending afterwards. In the home it is best avoided by adequate sulphiting of the extract, fermentation in a full jar under the air-lock, storage in a filled jar under a safety bung and the avoidance of equipment made of unsuitable materials.

Red wine pigments. Although the pigments of different red raw materials vary in their chemical composition, they all change to varying extents during storage of the wine. For example, the pigments of elderberry wine partially precipitate during the early stages of storage. Purple tints are lost giving the wine a richer red colour and softening the flavour. Longer storage, e.g. of red grape wine, changes the pigments from blue/red to red and finally to red/brown or tawny. The change is accelerated by light during storage so always store in dark jars and, unless the wine is to be entered into a competition dark bottles.

The reactions of pigments to such things as pH/alcohol/SO_2/air are very complex. Suffice to say here the judicious use of sulphur dioxide in making the extract and before storing the wine, give brighter red coloured wine, less subject to pigment browning and deposit formation. While free sulphur dioxide has a bleaching action, colour is restored when the SO_2 combines with some by-products of fermentation, or is itself oxidised.

Fine pigment haze in red wines can be removed by lightly fining with gelatin. Traditionally, commercial grape wines were fined with egg white. The white of one egg is sufficient to treat 70–90 litres/15–20 gallons of wine. Whisk the egg white with a fork and stir briskly into the wine which should clear within a fortnight at most.

• Microbiological Hazes

Non-deposit forming (non-flocculent) yeasts. Probably caused by a 'wild' fermenting yeast, fermenting the wine because of inadequate acid and/or SO_2 and/or no wine yeast having been added.

A sample of the wine does not give a positive reaction with any of the tests previously detailed, but does filter easily using a filter aid (page 13) or can be fined with Bentonite (page 26).

Lactic acid bacteria. The wine has a characteristic silky sheen when the holding jar is swirled and viewed against the light. The action of these bacteria is beneficial in acid wines which, if not blended, should be stored non-sulphited to give the malo-lactic fermentation (page 41) time to take place. But, in low acid wines, some strains of the bacteria can produce off-flavours which, if too unpleasant (e.g. mousiness), cause the wine to be thrown away. Sometimes a condition can also develop in such wines, called oiliness or ropiness, without serious flavour change. Then the disorded wine pours like light lubricating oil, due to polysaccharides produced by the bacteria. They also hold fine particles in suspension and make filtration difficult. The recommended amount of sulphur dioxide added to the extract, combined with a moderate acidity, will prevent oiliness developing.

Should a stored wine have a silky sheen or be oily, it should be treated with two Campden tablets per 5 litres/1 gallon. Sometimes the wine will clarify naturally after this treatment. If not it can be fined with gelatin and tannin or gelatin and kieselsol (page 26). After adding the prescribed amount of fining agent, leave the wine in a cool place until clarification is complete. Syphon clear wine away from the deposit.

Any equipment coming in contact with oily wine, particularly before it was sulphited, should be cleaned and sterilised thoroughly (page 14). Otherwise the infection will persist and other wines could go oily.

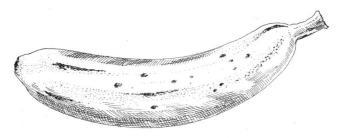

Yeast growth in a sweet, still wine. Characterised by gas pressure against the cork of the bottle, a slight haze and a cream or fawn-brown deposit. Decant the wine into a fermentation vessel and allow it to ferment. Stabilise as directed on page 44.

Vinegar bacteria. Stored or bottled low-alcohol wines, inadequately sulphited, and with some access to air, e.g. from faulty corks or storing bottles upright without a capsule, may show 'floaters' on the surface. In extreme cases these jelly-like strands coalesce into a thick, surface jelly plug. The growth consists of long chains of cells of acetic acid or vinegar bacteria. The wines should be drunk almost immediately.

• COLOUR CHANGES •

A white wine can turn brown, black or green shortly after being poured into the glass or otherwise exposed to air for a time. As noted under Hazes and Deposits above, there are two causes, either an excess of oxidising enzyme or the catalytic activity of excess iron or copper. Oxidising enzymes are usually derived from over-ripe fruit, while the metals come from equipment made from unsuitable materials. In both cases, exposure to air is essential before darkening can take place. Excessive amounts of any of these constituents can sometimes lead to opalescence or hazes.

The cause of darkening can be found by pouring some of the wine into each of three glasses. One is left as a control, to the second is added a crushed segment of a Campden tablet. A small pinch of citric acid is added to the third. The glasses are left overnight.
Obviously the control will darken, confirming the tendency of the wine to darken. If the treatment with a piece of Campden tablet prevents darkening, then excess of oxidising enzyme is the cause. The cure is to add one Campden tablet per 5 litres/1 gallon of the bulk of the wine. Should the citrated wine be the one to remain light in colour, then iron or copper salts are the cause of darkening. Addition of 3 g/1 oz citric acid per 5 litres/10 gallons will prevent the colour change, but not the unpleasant metallic taste if the two metals are present in more than a few parts per million. There are treatments for removing them from commercial wines but these are not really feasible in the home.

• PECULIAR AROMAS AND FLAVOURS •

At some time people have been given a glass of home-made wine which had a taste that did not please them. An injudicious mixture of raw materials or an unfortunate balance of sweetness, acidity and bitterness in the wine are easy to correct (page 40). Other unpalatable flavours are due mainly to the activities of spoilage organisms. This should not happen, since the principles necessary for making good wines have long been known. However, should they occur the methods for treating such problems are outlined below (see also Specialised Wine-Making Ingredients, page 24).

Vinegar. The obvious taint, mostly caused by acetic acid bacteria. These are found in rotten fruit or are carried from such fruit into the 'winery' by fruit flies. These organisms produce sulphite-binding compounds from the sugars in the juice or extract, rendering ineffective the added sulphur dioxide. When the fermented drink is subsequently exposed to air, the bacteria convert alcohol to acetic acid or vinegar. This is easily detectable at low concentrations in both the aroma and taste.

If the flavour is only just perceptible, add two Campden tablets per 5 litres/1 gallon. The next day mix the wine with freshly crushed raw material (or use canned, frozen or dried) of the type from which the wine was made originally. Use 1½ kg/5 litres or 3 lb/1 gallon, leave overnight, strain, add a large amount of actively fermenting yeast and re-ferment. One other possible source is a particular group of yeasts (*Hansenula* spp), again derived from poor quality raw material and inadequate sulphiting. These produce a compound of vinegar (acetic acid) and alcohol (ethyl alcohol) called ethyl acetate. This has the aroma of vinegar but not the acid taste.

There is one other little-known cause of acetification that occurs in the absence of air, described under malo-lactic fermentation (page 41). Acetic acid is produced when the lactic acid bacteria attack citric acid. The cure is to use malic acid for any acid adjustment if such bacteria become prevalent.

Hydrogen sulphide. The second major cause of unpleasant smells is the formation of hydrogen sulphide, sulphuretted hydrogen, H_2S or rotten egg smell.

This is produced by a combination of a juice constituent and particular strains of fermenting yeasts. The relevant compound is finely divided sulphur (e.g. as used in the form of dispersable sulphur on vines), sulphate, sulphite and/or a lack of the B-group vitamin, calcium pantothenate. The yeast is vitally important, since some strains, even though supplied with an excess of H_2S – precursors, luckily refuse to form hydrogen sulphide. It is essential to choose such a yeast strain or, if this is not known, the chosen strain should be discarded if it produced an H_2S taint. The affected wine should also be discarded.

'Yeasty' taint. There are some yeasty taints, rather like the aroma of freshly-baked bread, that are caused by the addition of excessive amounts of vitamin B, or by leaving the wine too long in contact with

the yeast deposit. Some yeast strains break down more readily than others. If a series of wines made with a particular yeast suffer from this defect, it is wise to change the culture.

'*Mousiness*'. A taint produced by a species of *Brettanomyces* yeasts or rare strains of lactic acid bacteria. The component responsible for the taint is unusual in that only about 25 per cent of tasters can detect it and find it utterly objectionable. The remainder consider the wine has a biscuity type of taste or are quite insensitive. It is found in low acid wines, made from non-sulphited extracts with some excess of air. If you are sensitive to the taint then the wine must be discarded since it cannot be removed.

Filter pad. Earlier filter pads or filter aids contained a material that gave an objectionable flavour to the first runnings from the filter. The practice was to discard such first runnings until the wine issuing from the filter had no taint. Now most filter pads and aids are acid washed. It is perhaps as well to check with a batch of filters from a new source.

All the aroma/flavour problems can be avoided by good hygiene, control of the amount of sulphur dioxide (SO_2) and acid (lowish pH) in the extract and exclusion of air, if no yeast is present.

INDEX

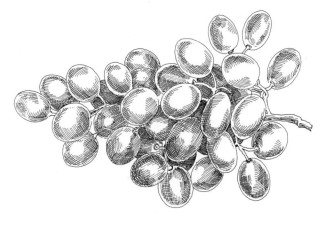

WHAT IS THE WI?

If you have enjoyed this book, the chances are that you would enjoy belonging to the largest women's organisation in the country – the Women's Institutes.

We are friendly, go-ahead, like-minded women, who derive enormous satisfaction from all the movement has to offer. This list is long – you can make new friends, have fun and companionship, visit new places, develop new skills, take part in community services, fight local campaigns, become a WI market producer, and play an active role in an organisation which has a national voice.

The WI is the only women's organisation in the country which owns an adult education establishment. At Denman College, you can take a course in anything from car maintenance to paper sculpture, from book-binding to yoga, or word processing to the martial arts.

All you need to do to join is write to us here at the **National Federation of Women's Institutes, 39 Eccleston Street, London SW1W 9NT**, or telephone 01-730 7212, and we will put you in touch with WIs in your immediate locality.

About the author

Dr F.W. Beech spent 36 years at Long Ashton Research Station, near Bristol, researching fruit juices, yeasts and cider and wine fermentations. He was also responsible for advisory work on these subjects. In the 1970s he was head of the Food and Beverage Division and Deputy Director. He has written or been co-author of four books on home wine-making, including the original NFWI *Home-made Wines, Syrups & Cordials*, and over 75 scientific and advisory publications on these subjects.